A New
LIFE

A New
LIFE

Your Connection to Christ

———————————Angela Camon

 www.trafford.com

North America & international
toll-free: 1 888 232 4444 (USA & Canada)
fax: 812 355 4082

Contents

Dedication

I dedicate this book to every born again believer who has made Jesus their Lord and Savior. It is also dedicated to those who have received encouragement by reading this book and as a result have made a decision to connect with Jesus and accept the new life that only He can offer.

Acknowledgments

I give thanks to God for this opportunity. To my husband, Carl I love you honey, thanks for all your support, love and encouragement. To my four children, Carl Jr., Aaron, Camille and Candace, I love you all. Thanks for being supportive. To my parents, Rev. Dr. Vickery F. Williams and the late Pauline F. Williams. To my sisters, Tracie Davis, Vickie Smith and Kyna Williams. I love you all.

Introduction

I felt compel to indulge in the topic of new life by sharing my testimony on how I made a connection with Christ and the difference it made in my life. I grew up in a two parent Christian home where the importance of getting a good education and going to church was instilled in me and my three sisters. Both of my parents being educators themselves, the question of whether my sisters and I were going to college was never entertained in their minds; it was only a matter of where we were going. They were passionate about all four of us going to college because they knew that having a higher level of education would open doors for us and take us further in life. My parents were equally passionate about us learning about God on a higher level as well. I guess that is why they had us in church what seemed like every time the church doors were opened. I can remember on several occasions leaving our house early on Sunday morning headed to Sunday school only to return home late that evening after have attended three church services. Throughout the week we attended bible study and any other activities that were being held. If any type of service was going on in church, you can rest assured that my three sisters and I were going to be there, even if we were the only young people there.

My parents were dedicated in serving God and as loving parents; they did what they were supposed to do. They kept me in church, and they made certain that I was taught the word of God. In fact my mom was my Sunday school teacher and my Bible study teacher, so needless to say the word of God was ingrained in me. But the fact of the matter was I was in church, and I was constantly hearing the word of God, but I was still was not saved. Although my parents had laid the foundation for me to build a relationship with Jesus, I had not invited Jesus into my heart to be my savior.

The fact that I just had heard about Jesus and not experienced him, life for me was miserable. At the time, I couldn't understand why I felt sad all of the time. Looking from the inside out, it would seem that I would be content. My basic essential needs in my life were met. I never went to bed hungry because I had food to eat. I always had clothes to wear. I live in a house with two parents who loved me. I had three sisters, who for the most part I got along with. I had friends who I enjoyed hanging out with. But there was still something missing in my life. I had a big empty hole in my heart. I had a void in my life and nothing that I tried to fill it with ever worked. My family could not fill the void. My friends could not fill the void. Even the church activities that I was involved in could not fill the void.

My mind was never at peace. There was always a constant battle going on inside of me. Everything that I tried to do seemed to always fail. I did not have the success that other people were experiencing in their lives. That was because I was trying to do things in my own strength. I didn't have Jesus on my side.

I came to a point in my life where I hit rock bottom. I was at my lowest point in my life. The devil knew that and he took advantage of that. He kept feeding me the lies that I was worthless and my life was not worth living. Some of life experiences sent me spiraling into a black cloud of hopelessness with the seemingly inability to recover.

I grew tired of this life as I knew it. I was tired of feeling empty. I was tired of living life without knowing my purpose. I knew that I needed Jesus. I decided to invite him into my heart.

After I received Jesus my life changed for the better. Where my life was filled with anxiety and turmoil, I had a peace that surpassed all understanding. I felt a love in a way that I had never felt before. Most importantly, as I studied the word of God, I grew in my relationship with Jesus. That emptiness that I once felt was replaced with his unconditional love. Some of the things that I once had failed at, I was now successful. I had a new life. Now I don't mean to portray that this new life that I had was something magical or super real, because that is nothing of the sort, but there was a difference in my life. I was a new creature.

There are some people who may have a more interesting testimony than mine. In fact some of my friends have shared with me the lifestyle that they lived before they came to know Jesus as Lord and Savior. Some of them were involved in partying, drinking, smoking, fornicating and anything else that they were led by Satan to get involved in. I on the other hand didn't party and drink and do the types of things that would be considered worldly. I was a church girl. I was a preacher's kid. I grew up in the church. But still I was no different than my friends. We all needed Jesus.

The purpose of sharing my testimony is to emphasize the point that even though you may have grown up in a Christian home like I did, if you have not invited Jesus into your heart, then you are not saved. It does not matter what point you are in your life, whether you are living a life of respect for God in the highest regard or whether you have made a litany of mistakes. You can be a "good person" who has done all of the "right" things or you could be the person who has committed every sin known to man, either way you still need Jesus. It does not matter how educated or uneducated you are, it doesn't matter about your demographical location, it doesn't matter if you are rich or poor, black or white, if you have not accepted Jesus into your heart, then you are not saved. If you are not saved, then you do not have new life because you are not connected to Christ. Making a connection with Jesus offers a fresh start on the path to becoming what God has ordained for you to be. It is the beginning to living a new life of peace and harmony and with the assurance of your eternal destiny.

Fill the Void
Chapter 1

But whosoever drinketh of the water that I shall give him shall
never thirst; but the water that I shall give him shall be in him
a well of water springing up into everlasting life. John 4:14

As I mentioned in the introduction, before I accepted Jesus into my heart, my life was empty. There was a dark and empty void in my heart. My life was meaningless without Jesus. Your life without Jesus is no exception.

God designed it that way. In every person's heart, there is a void; an empty place that was intended to only be filled by His Son Jesus. We were meant to have fellowship with our creator and to get our joy from him. Many people try to fill the void in their lives with other things such as money, drugs, careers, relationships, fame. This provides an artificial source of happiness because nothing can take the place of your relationship with Jesus. The inner emptiness that pervades many people's lives exists due to the lack of personal fulfillment with God. Some people rely on coping mechanisms like working too much, spending too much money, partying too much, drinking too much, in an effort to replace having an intimate relationship with God. Many people think they will find fulfillment by climbing the corporate ladder. They think that they will find it based on the world's definition of success. A friend of mine shared with me about the void she had in her life before accepted Christ. Gayle was a successful businesswoman. She had received several awards recognizing her accomplishments. One of her most proud accomplishments was being a recipient of the Business Woman of the Year award. She was happily married with three wonderful children. She and her family lived in a nice home in a very luxurious neighborhood. They lived a very extravagant lifestyle, as money was no object for them. But there was something missing. Even with all the accomplishments that she had achieved, there still seemed to be a void in her life. She tried to fill the void with drugs and alcohol. Drugs and alcohol became the band aid for her pain. With all other hope gone, Gayle finally came to a turning point in her life and realized that she needed Jesus to fill the void in her life.

Can you relate to Gayle? Do you feel as though something is missing in your life? Is there a void in your life? Have you been trying to satisfy that gnawing feeling of emptiness with the superficial things of this world? Have you been seeking fulfillment through religious traditions or occult practices?

The void in your life can not be built on a foundation based on your family and friends, the security of your job, or on your material things that you possess. You can't try to fill your life with things such as material possessions with the expectation that those things will do only what a relationship with God will do. They may bring satisfaction momentarily, but these things cannot truly satisfy that inner longing in our lives that only Jesus can fill. The solution to filling the void in your life is to invite Jesus Christ into your heart. Only a personal relationship with Jesus Christ will truly satisfy the longing that you have for a sense of fulfillment. Jesus offers to each of us abundant life. John 10:10 says "The thief cometh not but for to steal, to kill and to destroy: I am come that they might have life and that they might have it more abundantly". An abundant life is a life that is not void or empty, but rather it is full and satisfying and full of meaning. In order to have access to this abundant life, you must first connect with Jesus and allow him to fill the void in your life with his spirit. Without this connection, there will always be a void in your life.

The Bible says in Isaiah 43:6-7 says "I will say to the north, Give up; and to the south, Keep not back: bring my sons from far, and my daughters from the ends of the earth; Even every one that is called by my name: for I have created him for my glory, I have formed him; yea, I have made him". We were created to give God glory. When we live according to our purpose, our lives are filled with contentment, but when we don't live according to our purpose that God created us for, we feel incomplete and restless, and empty and alone. The reason that we feel that way is because God has made us for the primary purpose of having a relationship with Him. All other aspects of our lives are to flow out of our relationship with Him.

Jesus said in John 6:35 "I am the bread of life: he that cometh to me shall never hunger: and he that believeth on me shall never thirst". In this passage of scripture, Jesus was not referring to natural food and water, but he was referring the spiritual food that only he can give. Only Jesus can satisfy a hungry and thirsty heart. If you are hungry for true fulfillment, then open your heart to Jesus. He is the only one who can fill your life with so much love, joy, peace and happiness that you will never hunger or thirst again. I will say it again; a personal relationship with Jesus Christ is the only solid foundation that will ever fill the void. Nothing or nobody can take the place of Jesus. If you are living a life of discontentment, confusion, and brokenness, then let Jesus Christ into your heart and know Him as you Lord and Savior. He is the only way to truly fill the void!

Discussion Questions

1. Discuss some of the things that people use in an effort to fill the void in their lives?

_____

_____

_____

_____

_____

_____

_____

_____

_____

_____

_____

_____

_____

_____

_____

_____

_____

_____

_____

_____

_____

_____

_____

_____

_____

_____

_____

_____

_____

_____

_____

_____

2. What is the only source of finding true fulfillment in your life?

_____

_____

_____

_____

_____

_____

_____

_____

_____

_____

_____

_____

_____

_____

_____

_____

_____

_____

_____

_____

_____

_____

_____

_____

_____

_____

_____

_____

_____

_____

_____

_____

_____

_____

Your greatest decision
Chapter 2

I call heaven and earth to record this day against you, that I have set before you life and death, blessing and cursing: therefore choose life, that both thou and thy seed may live. Deuteronomy 30:19

The greatest decision that I ever made was accepting Jesus as my savior. It is by far the most important decision that you will ever make too. It is more important than choosing who you will unite with in holy matrimony, more important than buying your first home, more important than deciding when to retire. Whether or not to accept Jesus as your Lord and Savior is a decision which sets the foundation for all other decisions and affects not only your life here on earth, but it also affects your eternal destination. You have a choice of whether you will spend eternity in heaven or hell. The choice is yours but I believe that it always good practice to get all the information that can about a situation and weigh the pros and cons so that you make an informed decision. The same applies here. You need to know all the facts about God's plan of salvation and what it entails. God's plan of salvation is based on four spiritual laws. Just as there are physical laws that govern the physical universe, there are spiritual laws that govern your relationship with God.

The first law deals with God's love for you. **John 3: 16 says For God so loved the world that he gave his only begotten Son that whosoever believes in him shall not perish but have eternal life.**

The second law deals the sinful condition of man. Man was created to have fellowship with God, but because of sin, the fellowship with God was broken. Because of this broken fellowship, man was spiritual separated from God. **Romans 3:23 says "For all have sinned and fall**

short of the glory of God". **Romans 6:23 says "For the wages of sin is death, but the gift of God is eternal life".** The penalty for man's sin was death.

The third spiritual law is Jesus is God's only provision for man's sin. Jesus Christ said "**I am the way, the truth, and the life: no one comes to the Father but through me". (John 14:6)** Jesus is the only way to God. Jesus Christ died in our place. "**But God commended his love for us toward us in that while we were yet sinners, Christ died for us".** **Romans 5:8**. Jesus shed his blood and has paid the full penalty for your sin. God has made a way for you to be reconciled to Him.

The fourth law is you must accept Jesus Christ as your Lord and Savior. You must place your faith in Jesus Christ as your savior in order to receive the gift of salvation. **Romans 10:9 says "That if thou shalt confess with thy mouth the Lord Jesus and shall believe in thine heart that God hath raised him from the dead thou shalt be saved".** When you accept Jesus as your Lord and Savior, you are inviting him to reign, and be King over your life, thoughts and actions.

As I promised, we will look at the pros and cons of your decision to accept Jesus. Let me reassure you that the pros far outweigh the cons. I personally don't have see any cons in accepting Jesus as Savior, but for some the fact that once you make a commitment to accept Jesus, you can no longer be controlled by your flesh, but you must adhere to the commands and instructions of Jesus poses a problem. Some other reasons that I have heard used as an excuse why some people don't accept Jesus as their savior are they are not ready to give up the lifestyle that they are living. The enemy has deceived them into thinking that the life that they are living is the good life. They think that they are really having "fun", but they don't see the consequences that lie ahead.

Sadly to say, but there are some people who think that they are okay without Christ. They don't see the need to have him in their lives and feel as though they can make it without him. Some don't believe that there is actually a hell, so they don't see the need to be concerned about where their soul will spend eternity. But let me assure you that hell is real. Isaiah 5:14 says "Therefore hell hath enlarged herself, and opened her mouth without measure: and their glory, and their multitude, and their pomp, and he that rejoiceth, shall descend into it". I am quite sure that there are some other reasons that can be offered as a con to accepting Jesus as their personal Savior, but I would rather spend time focusing on what the pros or the advantages are for accepting Jesus. Some of the pros of accepting Jesus as your Savior are:

- *You can be in a loving relationship with Jesus.* John 3:16 says "For God so loved the world that he gave his only begotten son that whosoever shall believe in him shall not perish but have everlasting life". God loves us some much that he gave his Son, Jesus to die for us. There is no greater demonstration of sacrifice of love than this. John10:11 says "Greater love has no one than this, that a man lay down his life for his friends. While we were yet sinners, God demonstrated his love for us, so that we can have the opportunity to be in a loving relationship with Jesus.
- *You will be forgiven of your sins.* The Word of God says in 1 John 1:9 that if we confess sins he is faithful and just to forgive us our sins and to cleanse us from all unrighteousness. Forgiveness of your sins is available if you will place your faith in Jesus Christ as your Savior. Ephesians 1:7, "In Him we have redemption through His blood, the forgiveness of sins, in accordance with the riches of God's grace." Jesus paid our debt for us, so we could be forgiven.
- **You will no longer live in condemnation**. Once you accept Jesus as Lord and Savior of your life, you are released from the heaviness, guilt and shame caused by sin. Romans 8:1-4 says "There is therefore now no condemnation to them which are in Christ Jesus, who walk not after the flesh, but after the Spirit. For the law of the Spirit of life in Christ Jesus hath made me free from the law of sin and death. For what the law could not do, in that it was weak through the flesh, God sending his own Son in the likeness of sinful flesh, and for sin, condemned sin in the flesh: That the righteousness of the law might be fulfilled in us, who walk not after the flesh, but after the Spirit".

  At the moment of salvation, our sins are forgiven, or "washed away." As we read God's Word and allow his Holy Spirit to work in our hearts, we are increasingly set free from sin's power.
- **You will have peace and joy.** When we experience God's love and forgiveness, Christ becomes the center of our joy. Even when we are faced with trials and tribulations, the peace of God rests upon us. Philippians 4:7 "And the peace of God, which passeth

all understanding, shall keep your hearts and minds through Christ Jesus.

- **You will be in a relationship with God**. God sent Jesus, his only Son, so that we could have relationship with him. John 4:9 says, "This is how God showed his love among us: He sent his one and only Son into the world that we might live through him."God wants to connect with us and be in intimate friendship with him.

- **You have the assurance of spending eternity with Jesus Christ**. Assurance means "having been put beyond all doubt." By taking God's Word to heart, you can "put beyond all doubt" the fact and reality of your eternal salvation. 1 John 5:11-13 says "And this is the testimony: God has given us eternal life, and this life is in his Son. He who has the Son has life; he who does not have the Son of God does not have life. I write these things to you who believe in the name of the Son of God so that you may know that you have eternal life." You can have the assurance of eternal life only if you accept Jesus as your Savior.

Your decision to accept Jesus Christ into your heart can be the greatest turning point in your life. But you must make the decision to accept him for yourself; no one can accept Jesus for you. As much as I love my four children, I can't accept Jesus for them. I can lead and guide them to him, but ultimately it is a decision that they must make on their own. So it is with you, you can't be saved by someone else's faith. Will you accept Jesus as your personal savior by placing your own personal faith and trust in Him?

Discussion Questions

1. Discuss how your decision to accept Jesus or not accept him affects your destiny.

_____

_____

_____

_____

_____

_____

_____

_____

_____

_____

_____

_____

_____

_____

_____

_____

_____

_____

_____

_____

_____

_____

_____

_____

_____

_____

_____

_____

_____

_____

_____

2. Discuss some of the benefits/advantages of making the choice to accept Jesus as your Savior.

_____
_____
_____
_____
_____
_____
_____
_____
_____
_____
_____
_____
_____
_____
_____
_____
_____
_____
_____
_____
_____
_____
_____
_____
_____
_____
_____
_____
_____
_____
_____
_____
_____
_____
_____
_____

3. Discuss the four spiritual laws that govern your relationship with God.

_____

_____

_____

_____

_____

_____

_____

_____

_____

_____

_____

_____

_____

_____

_____

_____

_____

_____

_____

_____

_____

_____

_____

_____

_____

_____

_____

_____

_____

_____

_____

_____

_____

_____

_____

_____

Don't Wait Too Late
Chapter 3

But of that day and hour knoweth no man, no, not the angels of heaven, but my Father only. Matthew 24:36

One of the greatest lies that Satan wants you *to* believe is that you have all the time in the world to get saved so there is no need to be in a hurry. There that there is no sense of urgency. There is no time limit. When in fact, the Bible teaches us that time is at hand.

There was a story that I heard about Satan and his angels. Satan and his angels came together in a strategy meeting to figure out how they could fool more people into thinking that they had time, how they can convince more people to follow them, how they can destroy more souls. The first demon raises his hand, "I know, we'll scare them with something!" "Ah, no, that's been done," Satan says. "How about drugs and alcohol?" says another. Satan shakes his head, "We're doing that and it's been pretty effective. We have a good campaign there, but we need something more." "Sexual vices!" another demon says. "Yeah, that's pretty good," Satan agrees, "and we'll do some of that as well, but there has to be something else—something that virtually *everyone* will succumb to." Finally one particularly crafty demon raises his hand and says, "I know what we'll do: we'll just tell people that *there's no hurry!*" Satan laughs with delight. "Perfect!" he says.

Many times we make promises that once we reach a certain milestone in our lives, then we will give our hearts to Jesus. I have heard young people say that when they graduate from high school, they will get saved. But sometimes, it may be too late.

My friend Jesus is coming back one day. The bible tells us in Matthew 25:13 to"Watch therefore, for ye know neither the day nor the hour wherein the Son of man cometh". Mark 13:31-32 says"Heaven and earth shall pass away: but my words shall not pass away. "But of that day and that hour knoweth no man, no not the angels which are in heaven, neither the Son, but the Father". We don't know when Jesus is coming back, but we do know that he is coming. Now is the time to make preparations for his return. I reminded of a story in the Bible about ten virgins. Jesus used the parable of the ten virgins, also called the parable of the bridesmaids, to illustrate the need to be ready for his return. Jesus says "Then the kingdom of heaven will be likened unto ten virgins, which took their lamps and went to meet the bridegroom. Five of them were foolish, and five were wise." (Matthew 25:1-2).The wise bridesmaids took oil with their lamps, but the foolish bridesmaids only take lamps, with no oil. The bridegroom is delayed in coming, and so both the wise and foolish virgins fall asleep while waiting. Suddenly at midnight, the ten bridesmaids are awoken by a cry, "Behold, the bridegroom cometh, go ye out to meet him". (Matthew 25:6) All ten virgins rise up and trim their lamps. The five wise bridesmaids have their lamps ready, but the five foolish bridesmaids don't have any oil to light their lamps. The five foolish ask the wise to borrow some oil, but the wise bridesmaids refuse because there isn't enough oil to share. The foolish ones are instructed to go buy oil, and the bridegroom returns while they are gone. Jesus says in verse 10, "And while they went to buy, the bridegroom came; and they that were ready went in with him into the marriage: and the door was shut". The foolish bridesmaids came saying came also, saying, 'Lord, Lord, open to us.' But he replied, "Verily I say unto you, I know you not.'" Jesus then says, "Watch therefore, for ye know neither the day nor the hour wherein the Son of man cometh." (Matthew 25:13)

My friend, don't let this same thing happen to you. Time is at hand. Now is the time that you need to make preparations for Jesus' return. Don't make the mistake that so many others have made and say "Oh maybe tomorrow". Listen, my friend tomorrow is not promised to you. James 4:14 says "Whereas ye know not what shall be on the morrow. For what is your life? It is even a vapour, that appeareth for a little time, and then vanisheth away. Why not surrender your life to Jesus today. Time is running out for you to make a decision to accept Him. Romans 14:11-12 says "For it is written, As I live, saith the Lord, every knee shall bow to me, and every tongue shall confess to God. So then every one of us shall give account of himself to God". You have a choice to confess now and be saved or wait until Jesus comes and still and be lost forever. The choice is yours. Don't let it be said you waited too late.

Discussion Questions

1. What are some of the tactics and schemes that Satan tries to convince you to wait to accept Jesus?

_____

_____

_____

_____

_____

_____

_____

_____

_____

_____

_____

_____

_____

_____

_____

_____

_____

_____

_____

_____

_____

_____

_____

_____

_____

_____

_____

_____

_____

_____

2. Based on the parable, the ten virgins, why do you think that it is important to make preparations for Jesus Christ's return?

_____
_____
_____
_____
_____
_____
_____
_____
_____
_____
_____
_____
_____
_____
_____
_____
_____
_____
_____
_____
_____
_____
_____
_____
_____
_____
_____
_____
_____
_____
_____
_____
_____
_____

Accept God's Invitation
Chapter 4

Come unto me, all ye that labour and are heavy laden,
and I will give you rest. Matthew 11:28

Imagine how you would feel after the fact that you have gone through grave details to prepare for a banquet for your family and friends. You sweat tirelessly over the hot stove preparing the best cuisine. You even took the time to decorate your home to elicit a welcoming environment. After completing everything and having every intricate detail in order, you extend an invitation to your family and friends to come to your house for dinner. Instead of graciously accepting your invitation, they each offer you one excuse after another as to why they could not come to the dinner party.

This is what happened in the parable of the Great Banquet. In Luke chapter 14:15-23 a certain man had prepared a banquet and invited many guests. Each of his guests made excuses as to why they could not come. The first guest said "I just brought a field and I must go and see it". The second guest's excuse was he had bought five yoke of oxen and he was on his way to try them out. The third excuse was offered by the guest who had just gotten married and couldn't come.

They all made excuses as to why they could not attend the banquet, much like some people do when the invitation to salvation is being offered. They can give all kinds of reasons why they won't accept the invitation. Some of the reasons that deter people from accepting Jesus' invitation are:

1. They feel as though they are not worthy of God's salvation. They may feel as though they have made too many mistakes for God to forgive them, so they reject God's offer.

2. Some people are sadly mistaken in their belief that they don't need a Savior. They think that they can live on their own strength and their own merit. They feel as though they don't need to be saved because they are "good people". They have the misconception that they can earn God's acceptance and make it to heaven based on their good works. I had a friend of mine who told me that she thought that because she didn't curse, steal, or drink and she was very nice and friendly to people, and active in her local church, that she was on her way to heaven. For years, she thought that she could get by based on her good works. It is takes more than being a "good person" to receive salvation. Eph. 2:8-9 says " For by grace are ye saved through faith; and that not of yourselves: it is the gift of God: Not of works, lest any man" should boast." You can't make it to heaven based on the good things that you do or the bad things that you eliminate. You must accept God's invitation and invite His son Jesus into your heart. Good works, good character and good behavior won't qualify you for eternal life in heaven. The fact of the matter is there are a lot of good people on their way to hell because they have not accepted God's invitation for salvation. Salvation is a gift from God. My friend if you reject his gift, not only will you remain separated from Him now, but when you die without Christ you will be eternally separated from Him in the flames of hell.

3. This leads to another point. Many people don't believe in hell. They don't think that hell is real. Isaiah 5:14 says "Therefore hell hath enlarged herself, and opened her mouth without measure: and their glory, and their multitude, and their pomp, and he that rejoiceth, shall descend into it". My friend, there is a terrible penalty for sin, and if you die in your sins, you will spend eternity in the flames of a burning hell. Revelation 20:15 says "And whosoever was not found written in the book of life was cast into the lake of fire. Revelation 14:11 "And the smoke of their torment ascendeth up for ever and ever.

4. Another reason that deters people from accepting God's invitation to accept Jesus Christ as their Savior is because they face the fear of social rejection or persecution. A perfection illustration of this is found in the book of St. John 12:42-43. There were many that believed but because of the Pharisees, they

would not confess Christ. They were more concerned with their status among their peers than doing God's will. Verse 43 says "for they loved the praise of men rather than the praise of God."

For some people, the things that the present world has to offer are more appealing than eternal things. Satan has a way of making the things of the world appear more enticing to the eye causing people to have their focus on the wrong priority. In Matthew 19:16-23, we read about a rich young ruler who was not willing to lose his earthly possessions in order to gain an eternal relationship with Jesus.

5. Many people simply do not want to surrender and give up their independence. Time and time again I have heard people make a vow that when they reach a certain milestone in their lives that they would come to Christ. They wanted to remain in charge of their lives and the way that they were living. They were not willing to take self off of the throne and place Christ as the head of their lives.

6. Another reason that is offered as an excuse as to why people are not willing to accept Jesus is because they like sinning and think that this is the best lifestyle for them. While they might not come right out and say that they like to sin, but their actions convey the message loud and clear. Satan has tricked them into thinking that they are having too much fun to give up the life that they are living. Satan has a way of making things look glamorous and enticing. He has a way of making you think that you are on top of the world, doing the things that you are doing, but in actuality you are not really living the good life until you have accepted Jesus as savior. Your life will be much fuller and happier when you are filled with God's love.

Out of all of the excuses that I have heard about why people don't want Jesus to be a part of their lives the most common one is because there are too many hypocrites in church. They have seen people who confess to know God but yet live a life as if they don't know Him. It is unfortunate, but things like that do happen. But to be quite honest, that is not an excuse. First of all going to church doesn't really have anything to do with you inviting Jesus into your heart. You don't have to be in church to invite Jesus into your heart. You can anywhere and he will hear you and accept you. Secondly, you are suppose to build your decision to accept Jesus based on what He did and not what someone else is doing or not doing. There are hypocrites in the church, just like there are like there are hypocrites on your job. There are hypocrites in your family. You don't disown your family or quit your job, do you?

Allow me to give you another reason that people give as to why they have not accepted Jesus. They are waiting to until they are older. In the previous chapter I talked to you about not waiting too late. I told you how dangerous it is for you to put off accepting Jesus because you might not have an opportunity to accept him later on in life as you had planned. Waiting until you get older is not a guaranteed thing. As much as we all want to live a long life, we are not sure that they will happen. Only God knows the number of days that we will live. Since we don't know, we should live each day as if it is our last and making the best decisions as we can. One of the best decisions that you can make is to accept Jesus while you have a chance.

Another reason that some people have not accepted Jesus is because they feel as though because they go to church that they are a Christian and that is good enough. But that can't be further from the truth. Going to church will not save you. That's like saying standing in your garage makes you a car or going to Mc Donald's makes you a hamburger. That is not the case neither is it the case that because you go to church that you are automatically a Christian. A Christian should go to church. You can learn how to be a Christian at church, but going to church does not make you a Christian. Accepting Jesus into your heart makes you a Christian.

There are many more excuses that I can share with you, but I will end with this one. Many people say that they are going to come to Jesus when they get their lives straightened out. My friend, the reality of that happening is virtually impossible that is if you are trying to do it on your own. Sure there are some things that you can work on to improve your life, but you will never be at a place where you are totally straighten out. You will never be a totally "good person". You will never reach a place where you have it all together and you are at the point where you feel that you have cleaned up enough to come to Jesus. So many people fool themselves into thinking that once they get over a certain hump in life or get rid of certain problems then they will come to Jesus. My friend once you get over that certain hump there will be another hump. When you get rid of that problem, there will be more problems, Life is filled with problems. I am by no means trying to depress you or make you feel bad. I just want to shock you with a dose of reality. You will never be "ready" to come to Jesus in the sense that you have worked everything out in your life. Your life will never be perfected enough to come to Jesus. But the good news is it doesn't have to be perfect. Your life can me tore up from the floor up, and Jesus will accept you. He loves you and wants you to come to Him just as we are. He is the one who will clean you up and get you ready for your eternal home in heaven.

The only way to be saved is to personally accept Jesus as your Savior, trusting in His death as the payment for your sins and His resurrection as your guarantee of eternal life.

My friend God is extending an invitation to you. He is inviting you to accept His Son Jesus Christ as your personal Savior. Will you accept his invitation or will you continue to make excuses?

If you have a desire to accept God's invitation, you can say this prayer:

Heavenly Father, I come to you in the name of Jesus. Your word says that whosoever shall call on the name of the Lord shall be saved. I am calling on you. I pray and ask Jesus to come into my heart and be Lord over my life. Romans 10:9-10 says "That shalt confess with thy mouth the Lord Jesus , and shall believe in thine heart that God hath raised him from the dead, thou shalt be saved. For with the heart man believeth unto righteousness; and with the mouth confession is made unto salvation. I confess that Jesus is Lord, and I believe in my heart that God raised him from the dead.

Discussion Questions

1. Discussion some of the reasons that deter people from accepting Jesus invitation.

_____

_____

_____

_____

_____

_____

_____

_____

_____

_____

_____

_____

_____

_____

_____

_____

_____

_____

_____

_____

_____

_____

_____

_____

_____

_____

_____

_____

_____

_____

_____

_____

_____

2. Discuss the parable of the Great Banquet and how it relates to way people respond to Jesus' invitation.

_____

_____

_____

_____

_____

_____

_____

_____

_____

_____

_____

_____

_____

_____

_____

_____

_____

_____

_____

_____

_____

_____

_____

_____

_____

_____

_____

_____

_____

_____

Born Again Believer
Chapter 5

Jesus answered and said unto him, Verily, verily, I say unto thee, Except a man be born again, he cannot see the kingdom of God. John 3:3

I pray that you said the prayer and made the decision to accept Jesus as your Lord and Savior. If you did, congratulations you are now born again. You have made the wisest decision you'll ever make. The angels in heaven are rejoicing right now. You are a child of the King! You have been adopted into God's family. God is your Heavenly Father and you are His child. You are now heir of salvation, and entitled to every covenant promise in the Bible. Because you have submitted yourself to the Lord Jesus Christ and allowed Him to take control of your life, your name is now written down in the Lamb's Book of Life. When you became a Christian, you became born again. Jesus spoke to Nicodemus about being born again. Jesus said in John 3: 3 *Verily, verily, I say unto thee, Except a man be born again, he cannot see the kingdom of God.* Being born again means you have a new birth and a new life in Jesus Christ. Being born again doesn't mean that you experienced a physical rebirth, but it means that when you accepted Jesus into your heart by faith, your spiritual condition changed. It means that your spirit man is recreated. Being born again refers to all believers having been regenerated by the Holy Spirit. Regeneration refers to the work of the Holy Spirit in the salvation experience that produces new life in the believer. It is the work of God through the Holy Spirit of placing in one who has faith a new nature capable of doing God's will.

Accepting Jesus as your Lord and Savior is the beginning of a brand new life in Christ, and as a new-born child of God, there are many important things you need to understand.

1. **You are saved by Faith**-Your salvation is based purely upon your faith in Jesus Christ as your Lord and Savior. In other words, salvation is not something that can be "earned" by how good you try to be or some religious act that you perform. Salvation is a free gift from God, and came as you simply put your faith in Jesus, His death and resurrection, and trusted him to forgive your sins and become your savior and Lord. The scripture says "For it is by grace you have been saved, through faith—and this is not from yourselves, it is the gift of God—not by works, so that no one can boast" (Ephesians 2:8-9).

2. **You're not saved by feelings**-Feelings do not prove whether you're saved or not. There may be times when you "feel" that God is close to you, and other times when you "feel" that He's not. But remember that He has promised to always be with you and never leave you, regardless of feelings (Hebrews 13:5). Always remember that the Christian lives by faith, not by sight or the feelings of our natural senses. The Bible says "We live by faith, not by sight" (2 Corinthians 5:7).

3. **You may experience doubts**-One of the tactics that the enemy tries to use against new believers is to try to convince you that you are not really saved. But don't buy into Satan's lies and deceptions! If you placed your faith in Jesus Christ, then you are saved, regardless of whether you feel it or not. God's Word promises, "If you confess with your mouth, Jesus is Lord, and believe in your heart that God raised Him from the dead, you will be saved" (Romans 10:9).

4. **You are forgiven of all your sins**-When you repented (turned away) from your sins, and asked Jesus to forgive you, Jesus forgave every sin you've ever committed. 1 John 1:9 says "If we confess our sins, he is faithful and just and will forgive us our sins and purify us from all unrighteousness."

5. **You're not perfect, just forgiven**-Being a Christian doesn't mean that you won't make mistakes, but it means that you are forgiven of sin. You are not perfect, so you will make mistakes.

But you don't have to let Satan or other people condemn you if you stumble or make a mistake. Romans 8:1 says "There is now no condemnation to them which are in Christ Jesus, who walk not after the flesh, but after the Spirit. God is a loving God and he is ready to forgive you once you repent of your sins.

6. **You are a New Creation**-At the moment you accepted Jesus, He came into your heart by His Spirit, and now His presence and nature lives and dwells in your heart (1 Corinthians 6:19). You did not merely become a better person, you were "born again" spiritually as a brand new person! Now you must learn to live your life according to the new nature of His Spirit inside you. The Bible says "Therefore, if any man be in Christ, he is a new creature: old things are passed away: behold, all things are become new"(2 Corinthians 5:17).

7. **You have the promise of Eternal Life**-God's Word says that when you place your faith in Christ, you are given eternal life. When you pass away from this life, as we know it, your soul will go to be in the Lord's presence to spend eternity with Him! John 3: 16 says "For God so loved the world, that he gave his one and only Son, that whoever believes in him shall not perish, but have eternal life"

8. **You have been made righteous.** Romans 3:24-26 says *"Being justified freely by his grace through the redemption that is in Christ Jesus. Whom God hath set forth to be a propitiation through faith in his blood to declare his righteousness for the remission of sins that are past through the forbearance of God. To declare I say at this time his righteousness: that he might be just and the justifier of him which believeth in Jesus"*. To be justified means to be declared righteous. It signifies the believer's judicial standing before God. There is no just cause in man to warrant justification but because of God's grace, his unmerited favor, is bestowed through redemption. Christ's death is the ransom. You and I were released on the basis of the ransom's being paid.

Christ's death satisfies the Father's righteous demands. Its benefits are appropriated only through faith in His finished work. This is how the propitiation was accomplished. God can remain just and still declare us to be righteous only because Christ has paid for our sin and satisfied His holy law. You and I have not been rendered guilty but rather pardoned. Christ has taken the sin on Himself and has imputed His righteousness to you and me.

All this simply means that you and I are made right with God by our position in Christ. Your sins have been removed. You are holy and blameless as you stand before God without a single fault (Colossians 1:21-22).

9. **You have been redeemed by grace.** The word redeem means to buy back or repurchase. **1 Corinthians 6:20 says "For ye are bought with a price: therefore glorify God in your body, and in your spirit, which are God's."**

When you are redeemed there is a change in your soul and your heart. Your soul is converted from a state of being lost to receiving salvation, from being distant from God to being in a relationship with him, and from being condemned to being made right with God. God takes our spiritually dead state and brings new life to us through His Son Jesus Christ.

10. **You are a child of God.** Ephesians 2:19 says "**Now therefore ye are no more strangers and foreigners, but fellow citizens with the saints, and of the household of God**". You have been adopted into God's family. You have been transformed out of the kingdom of darkness into the marvelous light.

The Bible promises eternal life to all who receive Christ. 1 John 5: 11-13 says "*And this is the record that God hath given to us eternal life, and this life is in the Son. He that hath the Son hath life; and he that hath not the Son of God hath not life. These things have I written unto you that believe on the name of the Son of God; that ye may know that ye have eternal life, and that ye may believe on the name of the Son of God*". Based on this scripture, you have the assurance of eternal life.

Being born again means new life. With this new life, comes new responsibilities. Now that you have accepted Jesus as your savior, you are born again, now what. What must you do next?

1. **You need to be baptized in Water**-At your first opportunity, you should obey the Lord's command to be baptized in water as a confession of your repentance and faith in Jesus Christ (Matthew 28:19). Baptism is the immersion of a believer in the water in the name of the Father, Son and Holy Ghost. It is an act of obedience symbolizing your new life in Christ and proclaims that you are now committed to Jesus. Water baptism in itself, (not to be confused with baptism in Holy Spirit) does not save you or wash away your sins, but is an act of your obedience in God's Word. It symbolically shows that you have died to the old sinful life, and have risen in the newness of the Life of Christ.

2. **You need to join a Bible based Church**-Fellowship with other Christians is crucial for you as a new believer because it allows you to draw strength from others who love God and are growing in their relationship with Him. You should join a bible-based, Christ-centered church in your area. You should attend church regularly so that your faith can be strengthened by the preaching of God's Word, and so you can grow spiritually. The Bible warns us not to forsake ourselves from church attendance, because we need the strength and encouragement it brings. Hebrews 10:25 says "Not forsaking the assembling of ourselves together, as the manner of some is, but exhorting one another" and so much the more, as ye see the day approaching. Church is where you can go to express your love, faithfulness, and worship to God. By attending church, you can learn how to be a Christian and get direction and guidance from spiritual leaders.

3. **Ask God to fill with the Holy Spirit**-We already said that the Holy Spirit was born in your heart when you received Christ and now resides in you. But the Bible also says that the Holy Spirit can "immerse" you with a special power for service, to enable you to live a powerful Christian life, and to be bold in your Christian witness and testimony. **"But you will receive power when the Holy Spirit comes on you: and you will be my witnesses in Jerusalem, and in all Judea and Samaria, and to the ends of the earth"** (Acts 1:8). To receive this special power, all we have to do is ask Christ to baptize us with His Holy Spirit, and He promises that He will.

4. **You need to tell others about Christ**-You may feel that you don't know everything there is to know about being saved, but you can still witness to others, by simply sharing your testimony. It is always good to tell other people about what Jesus has done in your life. It is important for you to openly declare Jesus Christ as your Savior and Lord to others, as it establishes the testimony of your faith. Once you have accepted Jesus Christ, tell someone. Don't keep it a secret. The Bible says that "Whoever acknowledges me before men, I will also acknowledge him before my Father in heaven. But whoever disowns me before men, I will disown before my Father in heaven" (Matthew 10:32-33).

5. **You must keep living for Christ**-You must understand that your salvation is based upon your "continued" relationship with the Lord. He has promised to keep you saved, as long as you keep believing and living for Him. As a new Christian, you need to grow in your relationship with God and deepen your faith, so that discouragements, temptations, or trials will never cause you to drift away from God. Remember, if you depart from the Lord, you also depart from what gives you the promise of salvation. The Bible says that Christ will one day present you before God, holy and unblemished. You must continue in your faith, grounded and settled and not moved away from the hope of the Gospel" (Colossians 1:23).

6. **You need to Pray every day**-Praying is communication between you and God. It is simply you and God having a conversation. Just as you should read your bible daily, you should pray daily as well. You do not have to wait and pray in church, you can pray anywhere at any time. In fact, the bible teaches us to pray without ceasing (I Thessalonians 5:17). In order to grow in your relationship with God, you must communicate with him on regular basis. Many new believers start by praying the Lord's prayer (Matthew 6: 9-13). That is perfectly fine if you choose to start by praying the Lord's Prayer. But you might also want to include in your prayer giving God thanks, petitioning him to answer your daily needs, and interceding on behalf of others. Prayer is vital to your spiritual growth. God is your Heavenly Father, and He wants to hear from you and have daily fellowship

with you. Not only does He promise to answer your prayers, but as you pray He will also provide guidance and spiritual strength.

7. **You need to read the Bible daily**-One of the many things that you need to do as a new believer is to **start reading your bible.** While there are many translations, it is best that you choose a Bible that is easy for you to understand. Also there is not a certain chapter that you must start, but I recommend that you begin reading in John. You should read your bible every day. Just like you need food for your physical growth, you need spiritual food for your spiritual growth. God's Word is your spiritual food, and you must eat (read) from it every day. Reading God's word daily will cause you to grow spiritually. The more you study the word of God, the more God will strengthen your faith, speak to your heart, and give you guidance and direction for every need and decision in your life. David said "Your word is a lamp to my feet and a light for my path" (Psalms 119:105).

8. **You need to live a Holy life**-As we have mentioned, Christians are not perfect. However, God wants you to "aim" toward perfection. That is, your goal must be to grow in submitting yourself to the new nature of His Spirit in your heart, follow the example of Jesus, and live a godly and wholesome life (Hebrews 12:14). 1 Peter 1:16 says" Because it is written, Be ye holy; for I am holy". As you grow closer to God, you will have a desire to obey him and do the things that are pleasing in his sight.

When you made the decision to become born again, you took the first step toward reaching your divine destiny and living a life of divine health, divine favor and divine prosperity.

Discussion Questions

1. What does it means to be a born again believer?

_____

_____

_____

_____

_____

_____

_____

_____

_____

_____

_____

_____

_____

_____

_____

_____

_____

_____

_____

_____

_____

_____

_____

_____

_____

_____

_____

_____

_____

_____

_____

_____

_____

_____

_____

2. Discuss some of the important steps that you need to take after you are born again.

_____

_____

_____

_____

_____

_____

_____

_____

_____

_____

_____

_____

_____

_____

_____

_____

_____

_____

_____

_____

_____

_____

_____

_____

_____

_____

_____

_____

_____

_____

_____

_____

_____

New Life In Christ

Chapter 6

Therefore if any man be in Christ, he is a new creature: old things are passed away; behold, all things are become new. 2 Corinthians 5:17

When you accepted Jesus into your heart, your spiritual condition changed. You became a new creation. Having new life in Christ, it is important that you understand who you are in Christ. Paul teaches us through his letter to the church at Corinth who we really are in Christ. ***II Corinthians 5:16-17 says "Wherefore henceforth know we are no man after the flesh: yea, though we have known Christ, after the flesh, yet now henceforth know we him no more. Therefore if any man be in Christ, he is a new creature, old things are passed away, behold all things are become new.*** What Paul was saying was that we are to no longer evaluate one another based on a worldly point of view. We don't base things merely by their external and physical appearance, but rather what is on the inside. Your old nature, which is dominated by sin, is replaced with a new nature that is under the influence of God's spirit. You are no longer defined by the old things that have passed away but rather by the new things that come from God. God sees you in a different light. You have a new identity.

God wants all of us to know our true identity, but unfortunately many people are confused about their identity. People spend a lot of time and energy trying to discover who they are. They go on quests or spiritual journeys seeking to "find themselves". There are some people who live their lives based on the wrong perception, rather than on who God says that they are. The reason that they have issues with not knowing their true identity is because they have a distorted way that they perceive themselves, perhaps due to past negative experiences or other people's negative opinions of them.

Another reason that some people are confused about their identity is because of Satan himself. His desire is to steal what God has ordained for you. Just like we are susceptible or vulnerable to identity theft in the natural, so it is spiritually. Satan wants to destroy your spiritual identity. John 10:10 says "The thief cometh not, but for to steal, and to kill, and to destroy: I am come that they might have life and that they might have it more abundantly". Satan wants to ruin your life by confiscating your identity in Jesus.

It is crucial that you understand that your identity is based on who God says that you are. It is not based on the type of work. It is not based on who other people says that you are. It is not even based on how you perceive yourself. Some people suffer from having a low self esteem. They don't think highly of themselves. I believe that one way to combat the issue of low self esteem and to defeat the enemy from trying to steal your identity, is to constantly remind yourself what the Word of God says about who you are and what you can do through the power of the Holy Ghost.

Here are a few confessions that you can meditate on and say to yourself every day.

I am made in the images of God (Genesis: 1:27).
I am a Child of God (Romans 8:16)
I am forgiven (Colossians 1: 13, 14)
I am redeemed by the blood of the Lamb (Revelations 5:9)
I am saved by grace through faith (Ephesians 2:8)
I am justified (Romans 5:1)
I am born again by the Spirit of God (John 3:3-6)
I am God's workmanship, created in Christ for good works (Ephesians 2:10)
I am redeemed from the curse of the law (Galatians 3:13-14)
I am a chosen generation, a royal priest hood, a holy nation (1 Peter 2:9)
I am God's temple (1 Corinthian 3:16)
I am chosen and ordained by Christ to bear fruit (John 15:16)
I am more than a conqueror (Romans 8:37)
I am a citizen of Heaven (Ephesians 2:19)
I am delivered from the power of darkness (Colossians 1:13)

I am a new creature in Christ: old things have passed away and all things have become new (2 Corinthians 5:17).

I believe that as you make these powerful confessions based on the word of God that the power of the Holy Ghost will illuminate in your spirit and thrust you into your rightful position as a child of God and you will know that beyond a shadow of doubt, who you are in Christ.

Not only is it important that you understand who you are, but it is also important that you understand what this new life entails. As a child of God, you have covenant rights which you are entitled to. A covenant is a solemn promise, pledge or agreement between two or more parties to carry out the terms that have been agreed upon. The first time that the word covenant was used was in Genesis 6:18. God told Noah that because of man's wickedness, He was going to destroy all of life on earth. Then God told Noah "But I will establish my covenant with you, and you will enter the ark, you, your sons, your wives and your son's wives". God was going to preserve the animal population through the ark that Noah built.

Throughout the Old Testament we find several examples of God entering in covenants with others. One good example is the covenant that he made with Abraham. In Genesis chapter 17:1-14, God said

> *And when Abram was ninety years old and nine, the* Lord *appeared to Abram, and said unto him, I am the Almighty God; walk before me, and be thou perfect.*
> *²And I will make my covenant between me and thee, and will multiply thee exceedingly.*
> *³And Abram fell on his face: and God talked with him, saying,*
> *⁴As for me, behold, my covenant is with thee, and thou shalt be a father of many nations.*
> *⁵Neither shall thy name any more be called Abram, but thy name shall be Abraham; for a father of many nations have I made thee.*
> *⁶And I will make thee exceeding fruitful, and I will make nations of thee, and kings shall come out of thee.*
> *⁷And I will establish my covenant between me and thee and thy seed after thee in their generations for an everlasting covenant, to be a God unto thee, and to thy seed after thee.*

⁸And I will give unto thee, and to thy seed after thee, the land wherein thou art a stranger, all the land of Canaan, for an everlasting possession; and I will be their God.

⁹And God said unto Abraham, Thou shalt keep my covenant therefore, thou, and thy seed after thee in their generations.

¹⁰This is my covenant, which ye shall keep, between me and you and thy seed after thee; Every man child among you shall be circumcised.

¹¹And ye shall circumcise the flesh of your foreskin; and it shall be a token of the covenant betwixt me and you.

¹²And he that is eight days old shall be circumcised among you, every man child in your generations, he that is born in the house, or bought with money of any stranger, which is not of thy seed.

¹³He that is born in thy house, and he that is bought with thy money, must needs be circumcised: and my covenant shall be in your flesh for an everlasting covenant.

¹⁴And the uncircumcised man child whose flesh of his foreskin is not circumcised, that soul shall be cut off from his people; he hath broken my covenant.

God entered into a blood covenant with Abraham. As a result of their covenant, Abraham believed God's promise to bless him. You and I are included in the covenant between God and Abraham, based on the scripture Galatians 3:13-14. The Bible refers to you as Abraham's seed or spiritual offspring because you are in Christ. As a child of God, you can rest in His promise to bless you because He is a covenant making and covenant keeping God. In Psalms 89: 34-35, God says *"My covenant will I not break, nor alter the thing that is gone out of my lips. Once have I sworn by my holiness that I will not lie unto David"*. God is not a liar. That means that He'll do exactly what He says that He will do concerning you.

It is essential that you understand about the covenant between you and God, but having an understanding about the rights that you are entitled to is essential as well. You must have knowledge of your rights in order to reap the benefits. Privileges that are not exercised are of little to no value.

Your covenant rights include but are not exclusive to salvation, divine healing, protection, deliverance, prosperity and favor. Referring back to the scripture Galatians 3:13-14, we have been redeemed from the curse of sickness and from the curse of poverty. That means we have the right to total prosperity which means living life with nothing missing and nothing broken.

You have a covenant right to come to boldly to the throne of God. Hebrews 4:16 says "Let us therefore come boldly unto the throne of grace, that we may obtain mercy, and find grace to help in time of need". You were once a sinner separated from God, and could not come in His presence, but because of the blood of Jesus you have that right.

Embracing who you are in Christ, your true identity, and having a clear understanding of your covenant rights is only part of what it takes to live a successful Christian life. It is essential that as a new born again believer that you implement the following things in your life daily.

1. **Die to your old selfish ways** and surrender your will to God's will on a daily basis.

2. **Read the Word of God**-Learning how to grow spiritually is a life-long journey which occurs as you read and apply God's Word to your life. 2 Timothy 3:16-17 teaches us, "**All Scripture is God-breathed and is useful for teaching, rebuking, correcting and training in righteousness, so that the man of God may be thoroughly equipped for every good work.**" In order for spiritual growth to occur, we must be taught, rebuked, corrected, and trained by God's Word. Then we will be thoroughly equipped for every good work. The Bible is your manual for living your life so you should spend time reading and meditating on His word daily. Making the Bible your final authority is the key to living a successful Christian life. Reading the word of God produces spiritual growth.

When a newborn baby is born, it needs a lot of care. Birth is followed by a process of growth and development and time. In the spiritual realm, your new spiritual birth goes through a similar process. As a new Christians you need a lot of care and a proper environment so they can begin to grow spiritually and mature in your Christian faith.

God wants us to grow so that we do not stay on the same level of spiritual growth that we were on when we were first saved. It is his expectation that we grow into full adult spiritual children. If we do not grow properly our spiritual growth will be stunted. Peter gives instructions on how to reach spiritual maturity: **1 Peter 2:1 Wherefore laying aside all malice, and all guile, and hypocrisies, and envies, and all evil speakings,**

1 Peter 2:2 As newborn babes, desire the sincere milk of the word, that ye may grow thereby. Don't stunt your spiritual growth by not reading God's word.

3.   **Maintain an Active Prayer Life-**As a Christian it is a privilege to talk to God. Every Christian needs a special time each day when he gets alone with God in prayer. Mark 1:35 says, "And in the morning, rising up a great while before day, he went out, and departed into a solitary place, and there prayed." Jesus realized the need to pull away for a while and get alone with His Father in prayer. Paul said, "Pray without ceasing" in I Thessalonians 5:17. Prayer is to be continual. We should pray with thanksgiving in our hearts, petitioning God for our needs and wants and also interceding on behalf of others. (I will discuss more about prayer in another chapter).

4.   **Fasting-**Fasting is one of the most powerful spiritual discipline in the life of a Christian. The purpose of a biblical fast is not to lose weight, but rather to gain deeper fellowship with God. Fasting allows you to take your eyes off the things of the world and focus completely on God. Although fasting in Scripture is almost always a fast from food, there are other ways to fast. Anything that you give up temporarily in order to focus all our attention on God can be considered a fast. (I will discuss more about fasting in another chapter)

5.   **Walk in the Spirit of God-**To walk in the spirit is being led by the Holy Spirit and allowing him to lead and guide you. Galatians 5:16-18, 24-25 explains, *"This I say then, Walk in the Spirit, and ye shall not fulfill the lust of the flesh. For the flesh lusteth against the Spirit, and the Spirit against the flesh: and these are contrary the one to the other: so that ye cannot do the things that ye would. But if ye be led of the Spirit, ye are not under the law. And they that are Christ's have crucified the flesh with the affections and lusts. If we live in the Spirit, let us also walk in the Spirit.*

6. **Renew your mind**-Our soul is made up of our mind, our will and our emotions. Our mind allows us to make decisions, draw conclusions, and reason. Romans 12:2 gives clear instructions on how believers should be transformed in a new way of thinking. "**Be not conformed to this world be ye transformed by the renewing of your mind**". As a believer, you will think differently with a new mind set. There has to be a shift in your thinking. Because we are a new creature we don't have to stay on our old life path. The ability to change our way of thinking, to develop new attitudes lie within each of us as we transform our minds through the Spirit and the Word. Our attitudes will line up with the Word of God and our actions will reflect the love of God like God thinks.

Just because you have accepted Jesus as your Savior, doesn't mean you will automatically think like God does. The only way that we can think like God is to fill your mind with the Word of God daily. David said in Psalm 119:15-16 **I will meditate on your precepts, and have respect unto thy ways. I will delight myself in thy statues: I will not forget thy word.** To meditate on God's word, you think about it over and over until it fills your mind and your heart.

7. **Operate in the Will of God**-God's will is revealed in His Word. As you study and meditate on the Word of God, you will learn about God's plans and desires for your life. God designed a perfect plan and purpose for each of our lives. His perfect will has been designed so that we can live a blessed life to the fullest. **John 15:7 says "If you remain in me, and my words remain in you, you will ask whatever you desire, and it will be done for you." Do not let this Book of the Law depart from your mouth; meditate on it day and night, so that you may be careful to do everything written in it. Then you will be prosperous and successful.—Joshua 1:8**

8. **Practice Living a Disciplined Life**-To be a successful Christian, you must be disciplined! In I Corinthians 9:27, Paul says: But I discipline my body and bring it into subjection, lest, when I have preached to others, I myself should become disqualified. If

you want to be successful, you have to discipline yourself. And it starts with your body. It costs something to be disciplined. It is not enough to say that you want to build a strong relationship with God, but you must use discipline to pursue Him. This might include you getting up early in the morning to spend quality time with God when you would rather be sleeping in your bed under your nice warm covers. It will take discipline to spend time studying and meditating on God's word instead of watching your favorite television show.

Discussion Questions

1. Discuss what having new life in Christ means.

_____

_____

_____

_____

_____

_____

_____

_____

_____

_____

_____

_____

_____

_____

_____

_____

_____

_____

_____

_____

_____

_____

_____

_____

_____

_____

_____

_____

_____

_____

_____

_____

_____

_____

_____

_____

_____

2. Discuss the covenant rights that you are entitled to as a child of God.

_____
_____
_____
_____
_____
_____
_____
_____
_____
_____
_____
_____
_____
_____
_____
_____
_____
_____
_____
_____
_____
_____
_____
_____
_____
_____
_____
_____
_____
_____
_____
_____
_____
_____

3. What scriptural reference supports you having new life in Christ?

_____

_____

_____

_____

_____

_____

_____

_____

_____

_____

_____

_____

_____

_____

_____

_____

_____

_____

_____

_____

_____

_____

_____

_____

_____

_____

_____

_____

_____

_____

_____

_____

_____

_____

_____

4. How does embracing your new spiritual identity impact your success as a new born again believer?

Prepare For Battle
Chapter 7

For we wrestle not against flesh and blood, but against principalities, against powers, against the rulers of the darkness of this world, against spiritual wickedness in high places. Ephesians 6:12

Once you are saved, there is a battle called spiritual warfare that must be fought every day. Whether you realize it or not, you have been thrust in the midst of a battle. This battle is not between other human beings but it is between Satan and his fallen angels. Satan's main priority is to stop your growth. He does not want you to be successful in your new Christian walk so don't think because you have made the decision to follow Christ that he is going to leave you alone. Actually the battle is just beginning. Ephesians 6: 12th verse says "**For we wrestle not against flesh and blood, but against principalities, against powers, against the rulers of darkness of this world against spiritual wickedness in high places**. This lets us know that this is not a physical battle, but rather it is a spiritual battle; a battle that does not end until you die. As an enlisted soldier in the army of the Lord, it is essential that we be ready at all times to engage in war with the enemy. You must be prepared to fight.

It is much like an army that is gearing up for the preparation of wartime. In preparation for battle, a solider is trained to know about their enemy; who their enemy is, *how* the enemy will attack and what weapons he will attack with, when the enemy will attack and from where will the enemy attack. The same applies to the Christian life. Understanding the dynamics of the battle and how we are to engage the enemy is vital to our success.

As spiritual warriors, we need to know who the enemy is and all there is to know about him, his tactics, and his capabilities. Satan will use any tactic that he can to keep you from winning the battle against him. His mission is to destroy us and make us ineffective in fulfilling the assignment that God has ordained for us because he wants to stop the Kingdom of God from advancing. Satan's tools are in full operation in this battle that is waged against us.

But the question is how does Satan use his tools to wage this war against us in hopes of conquering us? He attempts to defeat us through his well thought out plans of deception. He uses deliberate deception and lies to appeal to our old man and fallen nature. Satan engages in war in the battlefield of our mind. He attempts to set up strongholds in our mind. A stronghold is an area in which we were held in bondage due to a certain way of thinking.

But Apostle Paul tells us that we have the weapons that we need to overcome Satan's strongholds. 2 Corinthians 10:4-5 says "For the weapons of our warfare are not carnal, but mighty through the pulling down of the strong holds. Casting down imaginations, and every high thing that exalteth itself against the knowledge of God, and bringing into captivity every thought to the obedience of Christ"

Yes we are indeed in a battle between the Kingdom of God and the kingdom of darkness, but the good news is that God has provided everything that we need to defeat the enemy. We have what we need, but it is left up to us to use it. The real question is if God has provided everything for us, why are some Christians surrendering to the enemy?

I believe that some of the reasons why some Christians are not winning the battle against Satan is because:

1. They are unaware that they are in a battle—
2. They are ignorant about the enemy and his tactics—As a spiritual solider, you must be abreast of who your enemy is and the various kinds of weapons that he uses. Being unfamiliar with his tactics and goals will allow him to take you by surprise and bombard you with one scheme after another.
3. They are not prepared for battle-. Preparations must be made in order to be successful. In order to be successful, all elements of warfare must be taught and practiced. We will lose the battle against Satan if we only focus on the victory and success of the Christian journey.

Since we know that we are in a battle, and we understand that we are under constant assault, we must put together a battle plan. Each day Satan is devising plans on how he can tempt you and lure you into his schemes. The Bible says in 1Peter 5:8 says "Be sober, be vigilant; because your adversary the devil, as a roaring lion, walks about, seeking whom he may devour. That doesn't have to be you, if you use your weapons that God has provided for you.

In a battle, there are defensive and offensive strategies that are implemented to gain victory against the opponent. The same applies in a spiritual battle against our enemy. We have two different types of weapons. The one type of weapon is used to fight against the enemy with and the other type of weapon is used to protect us from the attacks of the enemy.

One of the offensive weapons that we have is our tongue. Our tongue is a very powerful weapon that can be used to bring "life or death." We must really watch what we speak over others and over ourselves. We want to use it to bring death to the enemy and all of his works. On the other hand, we want to use it to bring life to things that are of the Lord.

The word of our testimony is another very powerful offensive weapon that we have. When we testify about what the Lord has done for us, we overcome the enemy. He doesn't like it when we share with others about all the things that the Lord has done for us. Satan feels threatened when we share our testimony because it breaks the chains of fear, doubt, and unbelief that he wants to use to keep us and others bound which hinder us from receiving anything from the Lord.

The Word of God is another one of our offensive weapons that is quick and powerful. With His Word we can easily defeat the enemy. The enemy knows that His Word is true and that the Lord always backs up His Word.

When we speak the Word of God from our mouths it is a spiritual sword with which we can defeat the enemy with, over and over again.

The name of Jesus is a powerful weapon is which Satan must succumb to. The enemy has to yield to the Almighty Name of Jesus. **Philippians 2:9-10 says,** *(9) "Wherefore God also highly exalted Him, and given Him a name which is above every name." (10) "That at the name of Jesus every knee should bow, of things in heaven, and things in earth, and things under the earth."* There is nothing that can stand up to that name. Every time the enemy hears that name, he trembles.

Worship and singing praises to the Lord is another weapon that we have that confuses the enemy. The devil knows that when we sing unto the Lord that it dispels the fear that he fights us with. He also knows that the Lord is on our side and is helping us to fight and win the battle. *2 Chronicles 20:21-22 is a perfect illustration of this. It says, (21) "And when he had consulted with the people, he appointed singers unto the Lord, and that should praise the beauty of holiness, as they went out before the army, and to say, Praise the Lord; for his mercy endureth forever." (22) "And when they began to sing and to praise, the Lord set ambushments against the children . . . and they were smitten."*

The anointing of the Holy Spirit is one of our secret weapons of spiritual warfare. Isaiah 10:27 says, *"And it shall come to pass in that day (today), that his burden shall be taken away from off thy shoulder, and his yoke from off thy neck, and the yoke shall be destroyed because of the anointing."* The "yoke" is whatever the enemy binds you with or puts on you. It can be sickness, diseases, habits, addictions, fear, depression, poverty, and many other things that are not of the Lord. The anointing of the Holy Spirit breaks all the chains of bondage and completely destroys it.

Prayer is a powerful offensive weapon. Not only just praying, but praying in the spirit. Praying in the spirit gives our prayers power that allows us to touch the very heart and mind of the Father to move heaven and earth in response to our prayers. No matter what kind of problem or even the size of the problem that the enemy uses to attack us with, when we pray and ask God for His help or talk to Him about something that is bothering us, He comes to our rescue and breaks the attack of the enemy.

Our faith in God is a powerful weapon. Faith is spiritual substance which we use to walk out and to do something with in the natural. Faith is like our muscles that we use in the natural. The more we use our muscles the stronger and bigger they become. So it is when it comes to our faith, the more we use our faith, the stronger it grows.

Some of our defensive weapons that we can use is described by Apostle Paul in Ephesians 6:11-18. He says,

"Put on the whole armour of God that ye may be able to stand against the wiles of the devil.
[12]For we wrestle not against flesh and blood, but against principalities, against powers, against the rulers of the darkness of this world, against spiritual wickedness in high places.

¹³Wherefore take unto you the whole armour of God that ye may be able to withstand in the evil day, and having done all, to stand.
¹⁴Stand therefore, having your loins girt about with truth, and having on the breastplate of righteousness;
¹⁵And your feet shod with the preparation of the gospel of peace;
¹⁶Above all, taking the shield of faith, wherewith ye shall be able to quench all the fiery darts of the wicked.
¹⁷And take the helmet of salvation, and the sword of the Spirit, which is the word of God:
¹⁸Praying always with all prayer and supplication in the Spirit, and watching thereunto with all perseverance and supplication for all saints.

The time to prepare for spiritual warfare is now. We cannot underestimate Satan and become complacent or we will become his victim. Do not think he is haphazard in his plan and his effort. He has a plan, and he is out to make it work. That is why God has told us in 2 Corinthians 2:11, not to be ignorant of Satan's devices. God has given us this knowledge in the Scriptures so we can fight a good fight and come out victorious. Satan will never give up; he is always trying to pull you back into sin. But we have our weapons that are not carnal but mighty through the pulling down of strongholds. We have the victory over Satan.

Discussion Questions

1. Discuss the offensive weapons and the defensive weapons that you can use to win the battle against Satan.

_____

_____

_____

_____

_____

_____

_____

_____

_____

_____

_____

_____

_____

_____

_____

_____

_____

_____

_____

_____

_____

_____

_____

_____

_____

_____

_____

_____

_____

_____

2. Discuss the reasons that some Christians lose the battle against Satan.

_____

_____

_____

_____

_____

_____

_____

_____

_____

_____

_____

_____

_____

_____

_____

_____

_____

_____

_____

_____

_____

_____

_____

_____

_____

_____

_____

_____

_____

_____

_____

_____

_____

_____

3. What does the Word of God teach you to do to overcome Satan's strongholds(scriptural reference)?

_____
_____
_____
_____
_____
_____
_____
_____
_____
_____
_____
_____
_____
_____
_____
_____
_____
_____
_____
_____
_____
_____
_____
_____
_____
_____
_____
_____
_____
_____
_____
_____

Fight For Your Destiny

Chapter 8

*For I know the thoughts that I think toward you, saith the LORD, thoughts
of peace, and not of evil, to give you an expected end. Jeremiah 29:11*

Now that you have made preparations for the battle, you must put
your game plan into action. It is time to fight!!! It is time to fight for your
destiny!!! Your destiny is what you were created to accomplish while here
on earth. Dr. Tony Evans, the founder and senior pastor of Oak Cliff
Bible Fellowship in Dallas Texas, defines destiny as the customized life
calling God has ordained and equipped you to accomplish in order to
bring Him the greatest glory and achieve the maximum expansion of His
kingdom. God has a divine destiny for each of us to fulfill. Not only did
he create your destiny, but he customized it just for you. No one else has
your destiny.

We all have a purpose for being born. This purpose is greater than
your own personal fulfillment or even your own happiness. It extends
beyond your family, your career or you accomplishing your wildest dream
or achieving your greatest ambition. Your purpose is not a single act, but
it is a lifelong journey. Not only did God create you for a reason, but
he also decided when you would be born and how long you would live.
He planned the days of your life in advance, choosing the exact time of
your birth and the exact time of your death. Psalm 139:13-16 says "For
You formed my inward parts; You covered me in my mother's womb.[14]
I will praise You, for I am fearfully *and* wonderfully made: Marvelous
are Your works, And *that* my soul knows very well.[15] My frame was not
hidden from You, When I was made in secret, *And* skillfully wrought
in the lowest parts of the earth.[16] Your eyes saw my substance, being yet

unformed. And in Your book they all were written, The days fashioned for me, When *as yet there were* none of them" God designed in you a blueprint(purpose, plan, dream or destiny) for "all your days . . . even before one of them came to be. This means everything you are to do and be was planned before you were ever born.

Long before you were conceived by your parents, you were conceived in the mind of God. God told Jeremiah "Before I formed you in the womb I knew you: and before you came forth out of the womb I sanctified you, and I ordained you a prophet unto the nations". When God formed you, He deliberately determined what your race would be, what your gender would be, your height, your hair color, your eye color and every other feature that it took to make you who you are. He determined your natural talents and the unique personality that you would possess. He custom made you just the way that you are. He made you the person that He wanted you to be. You were created on purpose for a purpose. You are not a mistake. You are not an accident. Your parents may have not planned your birth, but God sure did. You did not catch God by surprise. You are God's masterpiece. Ephesians 2:10 says "For we are his workmanship created in Christ Jesus unto good works, which God hath before ordained that we should walk in them".

As a born again believer, you have everything that you need to fulfill your destiny, but we must be willing to fight to take possession of the resources that God has provided. God has a plan for each of our lives. Jeremiah 29:11 says "I know the thoughts that I think toward you, saith the Lord, thoughts of peace, and not of evil, to give you an expected end". We have an intended end, but you must be willing to do what it takes to get to that end. Each of us should be striving to hear God say "Well done, thy good and faithful servant".

But if you think that Satan is going to sit idly by and let you reach your destiny without any opposition, you are sadly mistaken. Satan will do all he can to try to stop you from fulfilling your purpose that God has predestined in your life. That is why you must consistently and effectively engage in war to defeat him in hindering you from becoming the son or daughter that God is calling you to be. One of the ways that Satan hinders a Christian from reaching His own destiny is to get his attention by following the path that someone else is walking. Each of us have been given a spiritual gift(s) that we should use to glorify God. Romans 12:6-8 says "Having then gifts differing according to the grace that is given to us, let us use them: if prophecy, let us prophesy in proportion to our faith: or ministry, let us use in our ministering: he who teaches, in teaching: he who exhorts, in exhortation: he who gives, with liberality: he who leads, with diligence: he who shows mercy, with cheerfulness".

It is so easy to get caught up looking at what someone else is doing and try to emulate them. But you should use whatever gift God has blessed you with and do what he has called you to do. God does not need you to be anyone else besides who he created you to be. Always remember a photocopy is never as good as the original.

We all have a purpose and a destiny but in order to reach the place where God intends for you to be, you must strategize and implement a game plan. You need a game plan so you can stay focused on the goal. When I think of opposition, I think in terms of football. The object of the game is to make a touchdown. But sometimes along the way you will have opponents to tackle to keep you away from the end zone. You have to have plays and strategies in order to make it to the end zone to make a touchdown. In order to make a touchdown for Jesus, or by making it to the end zone of fulfilling your destiny, you must first know what your purpose is. Many people fail to live out their destinies because they don't quite understand why they were created. The only way that you will ever know your purpose is to seek the one who ordained it, which is God. God is the creator and you are His creation. He is the designer and you are His design. You will never discover your destiny apart from God. Your destiny is tied to your creator. Think about it like this; a manufacturer does not design and build a product, and then ask the product why it was made, but rather the manufacturer tells the product why it was made. Oftentimes, instead of seeking God for their purpose, some people will attempt to come up with their own analysis of why they were created. They try to self define their own purpose for their life. They ask themselves self centered questions, what do I want to be?" What should I do with my life? What are my goals, my ambitions, and my dreams for my future? When you focus on yourself, on what you want, and what you think your purpose is for your life, then your real purpose is not revealed.

Fight To Win

We all have seeds of greatness inside of us waiting to be recognized and released, but you must fight to win the battle against Satan. So how are you going to fight to win? What are the steps in your game plan that you must take in order to fulfill your destiny? One of the first things that you can do is to write your vision. Habakkuk 2:2 And the LORD answered me, and said, Write the vision, and make *it* plain upon: tables, that he may run that readeth it. Proverbs 29:18 says "where there is no vision, the people perish, but he that keepeth the law happy is he". Vision gives your destiny inspiration and direction. If you are fighting for your destiny without a vision, you will give you the same results as trying to start a fire with a wet match. It won't work.

You should keep your vision before your eyes daily. This will help you stay focused on what it is you are pursuing.

Secondly, you should confess the word of God concerning your destiny. You need to know what God has said in His word about the assignment that he has given you. Confessing the word of God concerning your vision, allows the Holy Spirit to manifest in your life what God has in store for you.

Thirdly, you must remain committed to God. Your commitment to God is an intricate component to you fulfilling your destiny. Paul said in Romans 12:1-2 says "I beseech you therefore, brethren, by the mercies of God, that ye present your bodies a living sacrifice, holy, acceptable unto God, which is your reasonable service. ² And be not conformed to this world: but be ye transformed by the renewing of your mind, that he may prove what is that good, and acceptable, and perfect, will of God". Being totally committed to God requires all of you. If you want to reach your destiny, the world cannot have a part of you. When you belong to God, you will be transformed by the renewing of your mind. Being conformed to something is similar to what happens when a potter molds a lump of clay. The potter squeezes, shapes, and forms the clay until it conforms to what the potter wants it to be. If you are fighting to win, you must not allow the world's way of thinking or the world's way of operating to conform you to its standards.

An imperative part of fulfilling your destiny is to develop confidence in God, and to step out of your comfort zone. Perhaps someone may be saying "well what if I don't like the destiny that God has for me. To that

I would say that there is no greater destiny for you than the destiny that God has for you. God will use your personality, passion, talents, gifts, past experiences, both good and bad to equip you for the destiny that He has for you. So there is no need to feel uncomfortable when totally surrendering to God and the destiny that He has for you.

My friend it will truly be a travesty if you spent all your days on earth wandering from place to place, from relationship to relationship, from career to career without completing the mission that God ordained for you. You have a God ordained, Holy Ghost inspired destiny. Seize it. It's yours for the taking.

Discussion Questions

1. In your own words, what does the word destiny mean to you?

_____

_____

_____

_____

_____

_____

_____

_____

_____

_____

_____

_____

_____

_____

_____

_____

_____

_____

_____

_____

_____

_____

_____

_____

_____

_____

_____

_____

_____

_____

_____

_____

_____

_____

_____

2. Why is it important to strategize and implement a game plan in order to fulfill your destiny?

_____

_____

_____

_____

_____

_____

_____

_____

_____

_____

_____

_____

_____

_____

_____

_____

_____

_____

_____

_____

_____

_____

_____

_____

_____

_____

_____

_____

_____

_____

_____

_____

_____

3. How is having a fight to win mentality connected to your success in fulfilling your destiny?

_____

_____

_____

_____

_____

_____

_____

_____

_____

_____

_____

_____

_____

_____

_____

_____

_____

_____

_____

_____

_____

_____

_____

_____

_____

_____

_____

_____

_____

_____

_____

_____

Use Your Authority
Chapter 9

Behold, I give unto you power to tread on serpents and
scorpions, and over all the power of the enemy: and
nothing shall by any means hurt you. Luke 10:19

When you made Jesus Christ the Lord of your life, Colossians 1:13 says you were delivered from the power of darkness. The word *power* is literally translated "authority." You have been delivered from the power, or authority, of darkness and placed into God's kingdom. Jesus said, "All power is given unto me in heaven and in earth. Go ye therefore and teach all nations, baptizing them in the name of the Father, and of the Son, and of the Holy Ghost. Teaching them to observe all things whatsoever I have commanded you: and, lo, I am with you always, even unto the end of the world." Matthew 28:18-20. That power was given to you as part of your inheritance in Christ Jesus. You have entered into this position of authority because you are in Him.

When God created Adam and Eve He said "Let us make man in our image, according to Our likeness, and let them rule. (Genesis 1:26). This passage of scripture reveals that God placed mankind on earth to serve as His stewards over His creation. He placed us here and gave us dominion and the authority to rule. David said in Psalm 8; 4-6 "What is man, that thou art mindful of him? and the son of man, that thou visitest him? ⁵ For thou hast made him a little lower than the angels, and hast crowned him with glory and honour.⁶ Thou madest him to have dominion over the works of thy hands; thou hast put all things under his feet:

Many Christians give too much space for the enemy to reap havoc in their lives simply because they won't use their authority. Ephesians 4: 27

teaches us that we should not give place to the devil. The only way that the devil can come in our lives is if we let him in. We have the power to stop him in his tracks. Luke 10:19 says **"Behold, I give unto you power to tread on serpents and scorpions, and over all the power of the enemy: and nothing shall by any means hurt you"**. There is nothing Satan can do to us if we don't allow it. But if we are not aggressive enough and choose not to operate in our authority, Satan will defeat us.

I was watching a basketball game a few months ago. As I observed the game I noticed that some of the players were not as aggressive as they needed to be. They did not fight hard enough to keep their opponent from getting the ball and scoring points. They did not position themselves to get a rebound. They didn't appear to be hungry enough for the victory. Even when the ball was in their reach, they did not exert enough energy to get the ball. Instead they allowed the opposing team to get the ball and trample all over them. I found myself screaming "Just jump up and take the ball". I believe that is what God is saying to us concerning using our authority that he has delegated to us. He is saying "just jump up and take your blessing. Be hungry enough for your victory. Be aggressive enough for the fight the enemy. Be determined enough to fight for your destiny". Satan might pose as opposition to you, but you have the authority to overcome and defeat him. We cannot allow the enemy to tramp over us and get the victory over our lives.

The Bible declares in 1 Peter 5:8 **"Be sober, be vigilant; because your adversary the devil, as a roaring lion, walketh about, seeking whom he may devour."** This scripture serves as a warning to us that we should be aware of our enemy. He walking about seeking those he may devour. The key word is "may". The word "may" requires permission. The enemy cannot enter into our lives and devour us because of God's hedge of protection, but when we don't exercise our authority as the children of God Jesus Christ, then we are in essence giving the enemy the authority to enter our life and have free rein.

When Jesus gave his life on the cross as the ultimate sacrifice for our sins, he also redeemed us from Satan's power and dominion. Colossians 2:15 says **"And having disarmed the powers and authorities, he made a public spectacle of them, triumphing over them by the cross"**.

Satan is already a defeated foe. God has already broken Satan's chains off of us, but we still have to enforce his defeated status. 1 John 3: 8 says "He that committeth sin is of the devil; for the devil sinneth from the beginning. For this purpose the Son of God was manifested, that he might destroy the works of the devil".

We must use the authority of the name of Jesus to repel and drive Satan out of our lives and break his grip. One way of doing this is to create an atmosphere of praise and worship which exalts the name of Jesus. There is one thing for sure, Satan cannot stand is the name of Jesus.

You have the power and the authority to take the Word of God, the Name of Jesus and the power of the Holy Spirit and run Satan out of your affairs.

God has given you the power and the authority to stand against Satan and his destructive works. In Ephesians 6, the Apostle Paul describes the armor that we as believers are to wear in spiritual warfare against Satan. 10. *Finally, my brethren, be strong in the Lord, and in the power of his might. 11. Put on the whole armour of God, that ye may be able to stand against the wiles of the devil.*

12. For we wrestle not against flesh and blood, but against principalities, against powers, against the rulers of the darkness of this world, against spiritual wickedness in high places. 13. Wherefore take unto you the whole armour of God, that ye may be able to withstand in the evil day, and having done all, to stand. God has provided what we need to win the battle every time. The armor and the weapons that you need are at your disposal but they are worthless unless you take your position of authority and assume the responsibility to use what He has provided. It is your responsibility as a believer to put on that armor and stand against the devil. God will not put on the armour and fight Satan for you. He has given you the authority to fight. God expects you to take use your authority stand your ground and speak directly to Satan. James 4:7 says to resist the devil and he will flee from you.

Christ has already completed his part, and broken Satan's legal power over us. It is our responsibility to keep Satan in his place. Instead of allowing Satan to pressure us, let's use our authority to put pressure on him.

Discussion Questions

1. Why is it important to use your authority against Satan?

2. Discuss scripture references that support your authority over Satan?

_____
_____
_____
_____
_____
_____
_____
_____
_____
_____
_____
_____
_____
_____
_____
_____
_____
_____
_____
_____
_____
_____
_____
_____
_____
_____
_____
_____
_____
_____

Exercise Your Faith

Chapter 10

Even so faith, if it hath not works, is dead, being alone. James 2:17

According to Hebrews 11: 1 "Faith is the substance of the things hoped for and the evidence of things not seen". Faith is vital part in the life of a Christian because everything that we obtain from God is acquired by our faith. It is what moves the hand of God in your life and is the key that opens the door to the promises that he has for you. Everything that you will ever need or want is available to you in the spirit realm. But it must be transferred from the spirit realm to the natural realm. You need faith in order for that to happen.

You can have all the desires of your heart and accomplish any dream as long as you have your faith in God. 1 John 5:4 says "For whosoever is born of God overcometh the world: and this is the victory that overcometh the world, even our faith. Through faith in God, your body can be healed, your finances can flourish, your faith will remove limitations, hindrances, and any obstacles in your life.

Romans 12:3 says "For I say, through the grace given unto me, to every man that is among you, not to think of himself more highly than he ought to think; but to think soberly, according as God hath dealt to every man the measure of faith. Everyone has been given a measure of faith. In fact, the moment that you were born again you God gave you a certain amount of faith. But it is left up to us to build on the faith that He has given us. As a new Christian, you must continuously build on your faith through the Word of God. Romans 10:17 says "Faith cometh by hearing and hearing by the Word of God. This is a continuous process and not a onetime thing. You have to continue to hear God's word over and over again. You must keep the Word of God before your eyes and ears. Proverbs 4:20-22 says "My son, attend to my words; incline thine ear unto my sayings. Let them not depart from thine eyes; keep them in the midst of thine heart. My son, attend to my words; incline thine ear unto my sayings. Let them not depart from thine eyes; keep them in the midst of thine heart. For they are life unto those that find them, and health to all their flesh". To attend means to pay close attention to. We must pay close attention to what God says in His word. God told Joshua "This book of the law shall not depart out of thy mouth; but thou shalt meditate therein day and night, that thou mayest observe to do according to all that is written therein: for then thou shalt make thy way prosperous, and then thou shalt have good success (Joshua 1:8). The Word of God is what activates your faith. Without the word, the principles of faith become nothing but an empty formula. Faith is a spiritual force that works in the heart. It is the ability to conceive God's word in your heart. It is not enough to have God's word in your head, but you must allow it to permeate in your heart.

Faith is the ability to see in the Spirit what the word promised when it is not yet manifested in the natural. You must be able to see your prayers answered. Mark 11: 22-24 says "And Jesus answering saith unto them, *Have faith in God. For verily I say unto you, That whosoever shall say unto this mountain, Be thou removed, and be thou cast into the sea, and shall not doubt in his heart, but shall believe that those things which he saith shall come to pass, he shall have whatsoever he saith. Therefore I say unto you, What things soever ye desire, when ye pray, believe that ye receive them, and ye shall have them.*

This is one of my favorite scriptures in the Bible. First, it is because it is Jesus himself who is speaking and making a promise to all who believe. Secondly, I like this scripture because it applies to everyone. The only requirement is that you have faith in God. Thirdly, these verses teach us that our words have power. As long as you have faith in God, believe and not doubt, you can speak to your situation and it has to change. That means you can tell your body to be healed, command your problems to be gone, speak to your resources and they must come to you. All of these and anything else that you speak about will come to pass, if you only believe.

Jesus gave us a perfect illustration of this when he encountered the fruitless fig tree. He came to the tree, and the only thing that was on the tree was leaves. There were no figs for Jesus to eat. Mark 11:14 tells how Jesus handled the situation. Jesus spoke to the tree and said "No man eat fruit of thee hereafter for ever". The Bible says that the fig tree dried up from the root. We have the same power to do the same thing that Jesus did. Praise God we can speak to every mountain and it will dry up at the root. A mountain can represent any obstacle, or hindrance in our life. It can be a financial mountain. It can be a physical mountain. It can be a spiritual mountain.

Faith is like a muscle. The more you exercise it the stronger it will get.

Your faith must stay in activation mode. To activate your faith means to put it in motion or move to act. Faith requires action. The Bible teaches us about faith and works in the book of James 2:14-18.

14 What doth it profit, my brethren, though a man say he hath faith, and have not works? can faith save him?

15 If a brother or sister be naked, and destitute of daily food,

16 And one of you say unto them, Depart in peace, be ye warmed and filled; notwithstanding ye give them not those things which are needful to the body; what doth it profit?

17 Even so faith, if it hath not works, is dead, being alone.

18 Yea, a man may say, Thou hast faith, and I have works: shew me thy faith without thy works, and I will shew thee my faith by my works.

We must have corresponding action behind our faith. In other words you must act out your faith. I am reminded of a story in the Bible recorded in Luke chapter 5. In this passage of scripture, Jesus had been teaching to a multitude of people. The Pharisees and doctors of the law and people from every town of Galilee and Judaea and Jerusalem were present. The room was crowded. Every crack and corner of the room was occupied. The Bible said that the power of the Lord was present to heal them. That meant that the atmosphere was conducive for a miracle to happen because of God's power. I can imagine that is why the man which had palsy was determined to see Jesus. His determination as well as his faith is displayed when he came to see Jesus but could not because of the crowded room. Instead of giving up and going back home, his friends went on the housetop and let him down through the roof of the house on his bed right in the midst of Jesus. The Bible says that when Jesus saw their faith. He said, "Man thy sins are forgiven thee".

Jesus saw their faith because their faith had action. It was not enough for them to believe, but they demonstrated what they believed. You must act on your faith. When you do, according to the Word of God in Mark 11:24, you can have what things so ever you desire, if when you pray you believe that you receive then ye shall have them. It is important that as you are praying that you believe what you are asking God for, then and only then will you receive whatever it is that you are asking for.

For example let's say that you are asking God for a new house. You pray to God "Father you promised that if I delight myself in you that you would give me the desires of my heart. (Psalm 37:4). You promised to supply all of my needs (Philippians 4;19). I am asking for a new house. I take it by faith.

Not only have you activated your faith, but you have released it as well. Now you are in the position to claim the new house (or whatever you are believing for) as yours.

Your prayer now consists of thanking God for your answered prayer, in this case your new house. From this point on, you think and talk like the new house is already yours. You take possession of it. To take possession of something means to take ownership of, to lay claim of. You live like it belongs to you.

You must continue to take ownership of your blessings by continuously speaking God's word and by praying to thank Him for your answered prayer.

Sometimes Christians mess up and start to doubt God when things don't happen when they want them too or when they think they should. As faith people, we can't quit when things get tough. Galatians 6:9 says "Let us not be weary in well doing: for in due season we shall reap if we faint not". You can't get tired of praying to God. You can't get tired of speaking the Word of God. You can't get tired of doing the things that keeps your faith activated, and expect to get what you desire from God. James 1:5-6 says "But let him ask in faith, nothing wavering. For he that wavereth is like a wave of the sea driven with the wind and tossed. For let not that man think that he shall receive anything of the Lord".

We have to put our faith into action. Not having faith in God is a sin. Hebrews 11:6 says" ***And without faith it is impossible to please God, because anyone who comes to him must believe that he exists and he rewards those who earnestly seek him***".

Discussion Questions

1. As a new Christian, what are some ways that you can build your faith in God?

_____

_____

_____

_____

_____

_____

_____

_____

_____

_____

_____

_____

_____

_____

_____

_____

_____

_____

_____

_____

_____

_____

_____

_____

_____

_____

_____

_____

_____

2. What does the book of James Chapter 2 say about faith in action?

_____

_____

_____

_____

_____

_____

_____

_____

_____

_____

_____

_____

_____

_____

_____

_____

_____

_____

_____

_____

_____

_____

_____

_____

_____

_____

_____

_____

_____

_____

_____

_____

Use Your Gift
Chapter 11

For I say, through the grace given unto me, to every man that is among you, not to think of himself more highly than he ought to think; but to think soberly, according as God hath dealt to every man the measure of faith. Romans 12:3

At the time that we are born again, each one of us receives a spiritual gift or gifts given by God. A spiritual gift is a divine ability that is used to strengthen the body of Christ in order to benefit the kingdom of God. One of the greatest milestones that you can reach in your new walk with Christ is to discover your God given, Holy Ghost inspired spiritual gift. It is unfortunate but many Christians fail to maximize their calling because they are not aware of their gifts.

It is important to note that a talent is different from a spiritual gift. A talent is a human ability that people have at varying levels. A spiritual gift is ability that God gives to certain individuals that are designed to benefit His people and to advance His Kingdom.

Let's take a look at a comparison between talents and spiritual gifts.

Comparisons Between Talents and Spiritual Gifts

- Spiritual gifts are supernatural
- Talents are natural
- Spiritual gifts are received from God
- Talents are often inherited from a person's parents.
- Spiritual Gifts are received at spiritual birth
- Talents are received at natural birth.

- Spiritual Gifts are possessed by born again believers.
- Talents can be possessed by saved and unsaved people.
- Spiritual Gifts need to be exercised and require spiritual growth and maturity.
- Talents are fully effective when they are developed after years of hard work and practice. An example is an professional athlete.

God makes the choice of the gift or gifts that he wants us to have. Romans 12:3-8 says. **For I say, through the grace given unto me, to every man that is among you, not to think of himself more highly than he ought to think; but to think soberly, according as God hath dealt to every man the measure of faith. For as we have many members in one body, and all members have not the same office: So we, being many, are one body in Christ, and every one members one of another. Having then gifts differing according to the grace that is given to us, whether prophecy, let us prophesy according to the proportion of faith; Or ministry, let us wait on our ministering: or he that teacheth, on teaching; Or he that exhorteth, on exhortation: he that giveth, let him do it with simplicity; he that ruleth, with diligence; he that sheweth mercy, with cheerfulness.**

It is not up to you to choose your gift, but it is left up to you to use your gift or gifts. Spiritual gifts are given at salvation, but also need to be cultivated through spiritual growth.

Ephesians 4: 12 says "For the perfecting of the saints, for the work of the ministry, for the edifying of the body of Christ". According to this scripture spiritual gifts are used to prepare God's people for service and to edify the body of Christ.

It is important that you operate in the gift that God has given you. It is easy to get off focus for what God has called you because you are looking at other people's gifts and the assignments that God has given to someone else.

What are the types of Spiritual Gifts?

There are many types of spiritual gifts that are mentioned through the scriptures in the Bible. 1 Corinthians 12:4-5 says "There are different kinds of gifts but the same Spirit. There are different kinds of service, but the same Lord. Some of the spiritual gifts that you will find mentioned in 1 Corinthians chapter 12 are as follow:

Administration: Also called the gift of governing, the Greek word translated "governments" is *kubernesis*, the verb form of which means "to steer" or "to be a helmsman". This gift refers to the God given calling which empowers someone to *lead* in affairs relating to the Church.
A person with the gift of administration is a good strategic thinker, organized, has supervisory skills and manages people and projects well.

Apostle: The title apostle comes from the Greek word *apostolos* which means "a messenger, one sent forth with orders". An apostle provides leadership over churches and maintain authority over spiritual matters pertaining to the church.

Discerning of Spirits: The capacity to discern, distinguish, or to discriminate the source of a spiritual manifestation whether it emanates from a good or evil, truthful or deceiving, prophetic versus satanic spirit.

Faith: This is not the faith that is measured to every believer, nor is it "saving faith." This is special, supernatural faith given by the Spirit to receive miracles or to believe God for miracles.

Gifts of healings: The ability to supernaturally minister healing to others.

Helps: This gift has to do with rendering aid or assistance to those in need. A person with this gift may have a "spiritual burden" for the needy or afflicted.

Word of knowledge: The knowledge referred to is often said to relate to understanding Christian doctrine or scriptural truth.

Working of miracles: This gift is the performance of supernatural events that occur beyond ordinary human ability but rather by the power of the Holy Spirit.

Prophecy. To prophesy means to fore tell the Will of God to His people

Teaching: It is a gift given by the Holy Spirit, enabling one to effectively communicate the truths of the Bible to others.

Tongues: to speak in a language not previously learned so unbelievers can hear God's message in their own language or the body be edified.

Interpretation of tongues: This gift required that speech given in an unknown tongue be interpreted in the common language of the gathered Christians.

Word of wisdom: The ability to apply knowledge to make spiritual truths relevant and practical in proper decision making situations.

Another scripture that tells us about spiritual gifts is Romans chapter 12. These gifts include

Service: The word translated as "ministry" is *diakonia*, which can also be translated "service. There are many types of ministries and service to the Church, therefore the gift of service can be an array of gifts rather than just one single gift.

Exhortation: The ability to encourage Christians "to patient endurance, brotherly love, and good works".

Giving: Those with this gift share their own possessions with others with extraordinary generosity. While all Christians should be givers, those possessing this gift will go beyond this normal giving.

Leading: The spiritual gift of leadership is given by God to men and women who are set over others to help the church to grow and thrive beyond the current generation.

Mercy: This gift is identical to the gift of helps. It addresses physical, emotional, financial, or spiritual needs of others through, self-sacrificial love and service.

Ephesians chapter 4 is another scripture that addresses the topic of spiritual gifts.

Apostle: The title apostle comes from the Greek word *apostolos* which means "a messenger, one sent forth with orders". An apostle provides leadership over churches and maintain authority over spiritual matters pertaining to the church

Evangelism: The gift of evangelism is the ability and desire to boldly and clearly communicate the gospel of Jesus Christ so that non-Christians can become Christians.

Pastor: This term derives from a Greek word for "shepherd". Pastors are gifted to lead, guide, and set an example for other Christians. He or she is responsible for spiritually caring for, protecting, guiding and feeding a group of believers who have been assigned to their care.

Prophet:. The English word *prophet* comes from the Greek word *prophetes*, which can mean "one who speaks forth" or "advocate." A prophet interprets the divine will and commands of God.

Teacher: Someone who devotes his or her life to preaching and teaching the Christian faith.

The best way to determine your spiritual gift is to consult God. You should spend time with God in prayer and ask Him to reveal your gifts to you. He is the one who has endowed you with your gift or gifts.

There are various websites that offer spiritual gift test or assessments. Some people use these tests to help determine their spiritual gift or gifts. I am quite that these assessments are beneficial and can be helpful in guiding along to finding out more about yourself and as well your gifts, but please keep in mind no single test can fully verify "everything" there is to know about your spiritual gifts. That is why seeking God should be your top priority when it comes to determining your spiritual gifts.

Discussion Questions

1. Discuss the difference between a spiritual gift and talent?

_____

_____

_____

_____

_____

_____

_____

_____

_____

_____

_____

_____

_____

_____

_____

_____

_____

_____

_____

_____

_____

_____

_____

_____

_____

_____

_____

_____

_____

_____

_____

_____

_____

2. Discuss the various spiritual gifts that a born again believer can receive by God.

_____

_____

_____

_____

_____

_____

_____

_____

_____

_____

_____

_____

_____

_____

_____

_____

_____

_____

_____

_____

_____

_____

_____

_____

_____

_____

_____

_____

_____

_____

_____

_____

_____

_____

_____

_____

_____

_____

_____

Activate Your Prayer Life
Chapter 12

Be careful for nothing; but in everything by prayer and supplication with thanksgiving let your requests be made known unto God. Philippians 4:6

Prayer is communication between us and God. It involves us talking to God and listening as he talks to us. Prayer is the channel by which God's power can be released to meet our needs and to get involved in the affairs of our lives. The only way that God will get involved in our lives and the situations that we are confronted with here on earth is that we ask Him to. God will not intervene in your life or act on your behalf unless He is invited. We extend that invitation to Him through the process of prayer. In fact the essence of prayer is God can't do anything until we give Him permission. Yes, he has the ability to do whatever He wants to do, but He does not have the permission to do it. This might sound strange to you, but God needs your permission before He can do anything in the earth realm. Let me explain. Here's why God needs your permission. In Genesis 1:26, God said "Let us make man in our image after our likeness: and let them have dominion over the fish of the sea, and over the fowl of the air, and over the cattle, and over all the earth, and over every creeping thing that creepeth upon the earth"

God gave dominion over to man through Adam, the representative for mankind. As we learned in Chapter 10, Use Your Authority, the word dominion means to control, rule, or to reign.

It was God's intent that Adam exercise dominion that He gave to him, but unfortunately Adam relinquished it to Satan. Satan is known as the god of this world. He is in control of the world system. That is why the world is in a mess now. When God gave Adam dominion that meant

God no longer had dominion. That is why God cannot do anything in the earth realm unless we let Him. The way that we let Him or give Him permission is through prayer. That is why prayer is of the upmost importance.

Prayer is one of the many benefits that each of us as believers are entitled to. May I submit to you that you are living beneath your privilege if you don't exercise your right and go to God in prayer. My friend I count it an honor to have the opportunity to go directly to the throne of God for myself. It is encouraging to me to know that I can talk to my Father at anytime, anywhere, and about anything. Even when I don't have anyone else to talk to, I can always talk to God.

According to 1Thessalonians 5:17, we are commanded to pray without ceasing. That simply means that we are to continually be in prayer. We can be in prayer throughout the day, expressing and demonstrating our love and devotion to God. It does not necessarily mean that you have to be off by yourself in seclusion. You can communicate with God while you are driving to work, or while you are doing your house chores. You can whisper a prayer to God anytime.

We have a right to go to God, but some people only want to exercise that right when it is convenient for them. Too often people use prayer as opportunity to give God their "grocery list". But praying to God involves more than just telling God about the things that you need or the problems that you are having. It is not a time to beg or whine to God, but it is an opportunity to give him thanks and praise for the things that he has done for you.

Coming before God with a clean heart is essential to having a successful prayer life. We should make certain that our hearts are clean by repenting of any unconfessed sins in our lives before we go to God in prayer. Having sin in our hearts will hinder God from answering our prayers. David said in Psalm 66:18 says "If I regard iniquity in my heart, the Lord will not hear me. But verily God hath heard me: he hath attended to the voice of my prayer. If we want God to hear our prayers, then we must conduct a spiritual checkup to examine the condition of our hearts. We need to make certain that we are not harboring any unconfessed sins such as an unforgiving spirit. Let's take a look at Mark 11:25 to see what Jesus has to say about forgiveness. It says "And when ye stand praying forgive, if ye have ought against any; that your Father also which is in heaven may forgive your trespasses. Now these verses are speaking about forgiveness, but unforgiveness is one of the many reasons that prayers are hindered. There are several other reasons why our prayers can go unanswered. Take a look at

1. Proverbs 1:28-30-Then shall they call upon me, but I will not answer: they shall seek me early, but they shall not find me: For that they hated knowledge, and did not choose the fear of the Lord. They would none of my counsel; they despised all of my reproof. (Indifference)
2. Proverbs 21:13-Whoso stoppeth his ears at the cry of the poor, he also shall cry himself, but shall not be heard. (Neglect of mercy)
3. Proverbs 28:9-He that turneth away his ear from hearing the law, even his prayer shall be abomination. (Despising the law)
4. Isaiah 1:15-"And when ye spread forth your hands, I will hide mine eyes from you: yea, when ye make many prayers, I will not hear: your hands are full of blood. (Blood guiltiness)
5. Micah 3:4-"Then shall they cry unto the Lord, but he will not hear them: he will even hide his face from them at that time, as they have behaved themselves ill in their doings. (Iniquity).
6. Zechariah 7:13-"Therefore it is to come to pass that as he cried, and they would not hear; so they cried, and I would not hear saith the Lord of hosts." (Stubborness)
7. James 1:6-7 "But let him ask in faith, nothing wavering. For he that wavereth is like a wave of the sea driven with the wind and tossed. For let not that man think that he shall receive anything of the Lord. (Instability)
8. James 4:6-" Ye ask, and receive not, because ye ask amiss, that ye may consume it upon your lusts". (Self-Indulgence)
9. 1 Samuel 14:37 "And Saul asked counsel of God, Shall I go down after the Philistines? Wilt thou deliver them into the hand of Israel? But he answered him not that day". (Disobedience)

As a child of God, you always want to be in a position so God will hear your prayers; not just one time or every now and then. You should get results from your prayers every time that you pray. That is if you are praying correctly.

What do I mean by praying correctly? To pray correctly does not constitute the posture in which you choose to pray. You may choose to bow in reverence in to God, or you may kneel on your knees or lie prostate (face down) before God. You may choose to close your eyes or fold your hands while you pray. Those issues are significant, but it is not what moves God to answer your prayer. God hears and answers your prayers when you pray in line with the Word of God. God does not move based on your need, but He responds to His word. God's word is what gets results in your life.

In order to pray correctly, you must understand the Biblical rules and principles regarding prayer. There are different kinds of prayer for different kinds of circumstances. Each kind of prayer has its own spiritual rules that govern it. It is important that you know the rule that governs the kind of prayer that you are using or it will not work.

Let's look at this concept in the natural arena and use sports as an illustration. We all know that the game of football, basketball, baseball, soccer and tennis are all considered as sports. But each sport has a different set of rules. In other words, you can't take basketball rules and play football. You can't take football rules and play soccer, not if you want to be successful. Different rules govern the various sports, so it is spiritually. Spiritual rules govern the different kinds of prayer. Let's explore the different types of prayer:

One type of prayer that we have access to is the **prayer of agreement**. This prayer involves more than one person getting into agreement in prayer about a particular thing that they are believing God for. This prayer affords us the opportunity to join forces by connecting together and petitioning God on one accord. Matthew 18:19 gives the rule which governs this type of prayer. It says "That if two of you shall agree on earth as touching anything that they shall ask, it shall be done for them or my Father which is in heaven". When we walk in unity and harmony, the power of agreement will be manifested in our lives. Using this power of agreement should not be taken lightly. You should not choose just anyone to enter in this agreement with. You should choose a like minded believer who is of the same persuasion as you are regarding the scriptures. Don't chose someone just because they are willing to agree with you, make sure that they understand the principles of the prayer of agreement and they understand what the Word of God says about whatever you are agreeing on. That is why you need to be in harmony with one another.

Another type of prayer is the **prayer of petition**—Both Mark 11:24 and Matthew 21:21-22 can be used as the scriptures that govern the prayer of petition. Mark 11:23 says "For verily I say unto you, That whosoever shall say unto this mountain, Be thou removed, and be thou cast into the sea; and shall not doubt in his heart, but shall believe that those things which he saith shall come to pass; he shall have whatsoever he saith. Therefore I say unto you, What things soever ye desire, when ye pray, believe that ye receive them, and ye shall have them".

Matthew 21:21-22 says Jesus answered and said unto them, Verily I say unto you, If ye have faith, and doubt not, ye shall not only do this which is done to the fig tree, but also if ye shall say unto this mountain, Be thou removed, and be thou cast into the sea; it shall be done. And all things, whatsoever ye shall ask in prayer, believing, ye shall receive"

These scriptures give us the promise of answered prayer. Not only do these scriptures give us this assurance, but so do the following scriptures:

1. Psalm 91:15-He shall call upon me, and I will answer him: I will be with him in trouble; I will deliver him, and honour him.
2. Isaiah 58:9-9Then shalt thou call, and the Lord shall answer; thou shalt cry, and he shall say, Here I am. If thou take away from the midst of thee the yoke, the putting forth of the finger, and speaking vanity;
3. Isaiah 65:24-And it shall come to pass, that before they call, I will answer; and while they are yet speaking, I will hear
4. Zechariah 13:9-And I will bring the third part through the fire, and will refine them as silver is refined, and will try them as gold is tried: they shall call on my name, and I will hear them: I will say, It *is* my people: and they shall say, The LORD *is* my God.
5. Luke 11:9-And I say unto you, Ask, and it shall be given you; seek, and ye shall find; knock, and it shall be opened unto you.
6. John 15:7-If ye abide in me, and my words abide in you, ye shall ask what ye will, and it shall be done unto you

The prayer of petition is always based on the Word of God. As you find a promise in God's word, meditate on it, envision it coming to pass and pray about it in faith. Jesus said that you must believe when you pray in order for you to receive. That is how we operate in faith.

The next type of prayer is the **prayer of intercession**. This is the prayer that you pray for someone else. One aspect of intercessory prayer is to pray about something or somebody in your own native language. In other cases there may be times that the Holy Ghost will place someone in our spirit to pray for, but we are not exactly sure what we are to pray for about. This is when we pray in the spirit. There is advantage to praying in the Holy Ghost. Those times that we don't know what to pray for, the Holy Ghost will intercede for us. Romans 8:26 says "Likewise the Spirit also helpeth our infirmities: for we know not what we should pray for, as we ought: but the Spirit itself maketh intercession for us with groaning which cannot be uttered. And he that searcheth the hearts knoweth what the mind of the Spirit is because he maketh intercession for the saints according to the will of God". Praying in the spirit builds us up spiritually. Jude verse 20 says "But ye beloved building up yourselves on your most holy faith, praying in the Holy Ghost".

Another prayer is the **prayer of praise and worship**. This is a prayer when you come before God with no hidden agenda other than to praise His holy name. You just want to tell Him how much you love him and how much you appreciate Him for who He is and what He has done in your life.

Our final prayer that we will discuss is the **prayer of consecration and/or dedication**. This prayer is where you offer yourself to God for His service. This is not about what you want to accomplish for yourself, but rather what you can accomplish for God. You are in the position to pray "Lord not my will, but let thy will be done". Jesus prayed this very prayer before He went to the cross. In Luke 22:42, Jesus said these words, "Saying, Father, if thou be willing, remove this cup from me: nevertheless not my will, but thine, be done".

We can have the assurance of our prayers being answered every time that we pray, if we adhere to the rules of prayer. It is essential that you understand that prayer cannot be reduced down to a formula, but basic elements should be included in our prayers. We should have adoration, which to adore God in worship and praise Him, to honor and exalt Him in our heart and mind and with our lips. In our prayer, we should allow the Holy Ghost an opportunity to reveal any sin in our life that needs to be confessed. Once the sin has been revealed, then we should confess it to God and ask for forgiveness. There should always be confession of our sins when we pray. Thirdly, our prayers should consist of an attitude of thanksgiving to God. We should be grateful for who God is to us in our lives, the benefits that we enjoy as a result of being His child. We should always have a heart of gratitude toward God even when we are facing problems and adversities.

Finally, another basic element that should be included in our prayers is supplication. This includes petitioning God for our own needs as well as interceding on the behalf of others. Philippians 4:6 says "Do not be anxious about anything, but in every situation, by prayer and petition, with thanksgiving, present your requests to God".

We also need to bear in mind that we can have the desires of our hearts if we believe. We have the assurance of answered prayer based on the Word of God. Some of the keys that can be implemented to help you get result to your prayers are:

1. Decide what you want from God and be specific about it. Find a scripture in the Word of God that promises you what you are asking for. Keep in mind that you may not find a scripture that will fit exactly what you are asking for. For example, you are asking God for a Jaguar, you won't find a scripture that specifically says that God will bless you with a Jaguar. But you can stand on the scripture that says "Trust in the LORD, and do good; *so* shalt thou dwell in the land, and verily thou shalt be fed. Delight thyself also in the Lord, and he shall give thee the desires of your heart.

2. Ask God for what you want. You must open your mouth and ask God for what you want. God is not going to guess what you want nor is He going to assume that you want a certain thing to take place in your life. There is no such thing as a silent or unspoken request. Matthew 7:7 says "Ask and ye shall receive, seek and ye shall find, knock and it shall be opened unto you".

3. Make sure that your thoughts line up with what you have asked God for. Satan will do all that he can to get you to doubt God and the belief that He will answer your prayers. That's why you must continue to feed your faith. Remember faith comes by hearing and hearing by the Word of God. It will be very helpful if you keep the Word of God before your eyes and ears. Keep your mind saturated with the Word of God. You can listen to worship music that draws you closer to God. You can listen to sermons from your local pastor or televised messages from other preachers. You can read spiritual books that are based on the

Word of God. All of these things will help keep your faith alive and your thoughts fresh and renewed.

4. Keep a visual of what you are asking God for. I like to use my imagination to visualize myself with the thing that I am asking God for. I see myself with the answered prayer. I suggest that you do the same thing. If you are asking God for a new car, see yourself driving that new car. I also like to make a "prayer board". I take a poster board and everything that I am asking God for I put it on my board. I find pictures in a magazine that represent what I believing God for. This gives me a visual of what I want and keeps me focused on being committed to pray until I get it.

Discussion Questions

1. Discuss the different kinds of prayer and the importance of each one.

_____

_____

_____

_____

_____

_____

_____

_____

_____

_____

_____

_____

_____

_____

_____

_____

_____

_____

_____

_____

_____

_____

_____

_____

_____

_____

_____

_____

_____

_____

_____

_____

_____

_____

2. What are the important keys that you should implement to get results to your prayers?

_____

_____

_____

_____

_____

_____

_____

_____

_____

_____

_____

_____

_____

_____

_____

_____

_____

_____

_____

_____

_____

_____

_____

_____

_____

_____

_____

_____

_____

_____

Don't Rob God

Chapter 13

Will a man rob God? Yet ye have robbed me. But ye say, Wherein have we robbed thee? In tithes and offerings. Malachi 3:8

The area of finances is a way to honor God. It is also an area where some Christians fall short. Many Christians allow the enemy to trick them into robbing God. Most of the time when we hear the word rob, we think about a person robbing a bank or someone breaking into another person's home, and taking their possessions. But not much emphasis is placed on the fact that Sunday after Sunday, people rob God. The bible says in Malachi 3:8-10 "Will a man rob God, yet ye have robbed me even a whole nation? But ye say wherein have we robbed thee. In tithes and offerings. Bring ye all the tithes into the storehouse that there may be meat in my house and prove me now herewith saith the Lord of host, that I will not open you the window of heaven and pour you out a blessing that there shall not be room enough to receive".

God requires that we give him 10 percent of our income. For example if you earned $100.00, you would give $10.00 as your tithes. If you earned $1000.00, you would give $100.00 as your tithes and so on.

Tithing is not just like paying another bill. God's money should come out first. God is to always come first, even before your bills, your savings, and even before your taxes. I believe that if you don't tithe off your gross income, you are putting the government before God. You are excluding him from that portion of your income and it won't be blessed. When you give to God first, this is an act of obedience and a demonstration of your faith in God. It is not that God needs your money, because he doesn't. But he wants you to give it so that he in return can bless you. In verses 11 and 12, there are seven blessings that God promises that he will give you if you are obedient to his command to pay tithes. The seven promises are:

1. God will open the windows of heaven" (verse 10)
2. God pour you out a blessing, that there shall not be room enough to receive it"(verse 10)
3. God said he will rebuke the devourer for your sakes.(verse 11)
4. He shall not destroy the fruits of your ground" (verse 11).
5. Neither shall your vine cast her fruit before the time in the field, saith the LORD of hosts. (verse 11)
6. All nations shall call you blessed" (verse 12).
7. Ye shall be a delightsome land, saith the LORD of hosts(verse 12).

Don't fall into the trap that so many others have fallen into. In my many years of being in the ministry, I heard people say that they could not afford to pay their tithes. To be honest they could not afford to not pay their tithes. The reason that they felt that way was because they were thinking from a natural standpoint. In their mind, all they could see was the light bill, the water bill, the childcare expenses and every other bill that they had, they could not fathom taking money out for God in fear that they would not be able to make ends meet. That is the trick of the enemy. He wants you to be in fear that if you pay your tithes, God will not meet your needs. But that cannot be any further from the truth. God WILL bless you when you are obedient to him.

Reasons Why You Should Tithe

1. **Because God commands it!**
"A tithe of all you produce is the Lord's and it is Holy." (Lev. 27:30)
2. **Because tithing shows that God has first place in your life!**
"The purpose of tithing is to teach you to put God first place in your life". (Deut. 14:23) If God does not have first priority in your finances, He isn't really first in your life. Proverbs 3:9 says "Honour the Lord with thy substance, and with the first fruits of all thine increase".

3. **Because it is an opportunity to express your gratitude to God for helping you earn income!**

We should be thankful that God that he has allowed us to earn income so that we can give our tithes and offerings. We must remember that it is God who has given us the power to get wealth (Deuteronomy 8:18). So rather than taking the attitude "I'm giving God 10% of my money, think about it this way, God is allowing you to keep 90% of His money. My husband often prays the prayer that God will cause increase in his finances so that he can pay more tithes. He wants God to give him more opportunities to give. That is the right attitude that God wants us to have.

4. **Because refusing to tithe is stealing from God!**

If you don't tithe, God says you are using money that rightfully belongs to Him. "God says: "Will a man rob God? Yet you are robbing me!' But you ask, 'How do we rob you?' God says: 'In tithes and offerings. Bring your whole tithe to My house.'" (Mal. 3:8-19)

5. **Because tithing gives you a chance to put God to the test.**

This is one of the most amazing promises in the word of God in which God challenges us to put him to the test. The word of God tells us to test God by bring all of our tithes to the store house and he promises to open the windows of heaven and pour out a blessing that we won't have room enough to receive.

Not only does he promise to bless us, but he also promises to keep and protect what we already have.

6. **Because tithing demonstrates your love for God!**

Matthew 6:21 says "For where your treasure is, there will your heart be also." In other words, wherever you put your money is where your affection is going to be. It's easy to say that you love the Lord, but you must put that love into action. One way of doing that is to give back to God. Jesus said in John 14:15, "If you love me, keep my commands". You may say you love God, but 2 Cor. 8:8 puts the sincerity of your love to the test. It says "I speak not by commandment, but by occasion of the forwardness of others, and to prove the sincerity of your love.

You can give without loving but you cannot love without giving.

Sowing seeds

It is God's will that you prosper and live the abundant life. One of the ways that God will lead us to a place of living in the overflow is through sowing seeds. God has a way that he operates in his kingdom. One of the ways is through the process of sowing and reaping or seedtime and harvest. This process is the basic principle for all of heaven's operations. There are several ways that you can sow seeds. You can sow seeds of your time, kindness, talent, the list goes on, but in this section I want to discuss primarily sowing financial seeds. According to scripture, God is the one who gives seed the sower. 2 Corinthians 9:10 says "**Now he that ministereth seed to the sower both minister bread for your food, and multiply your seed sown and increase the fruit of your righteousness**"

Isaiah 55:10-11 says "**For as the rain cometh down, and the snow from heaven, and returneth not thither, but watereth the earth, and maketh it bring forth and bud, that it may give seed to the sower, and bread to the eater. So shall my word be that goeth forth out of my mouth: it shall not return unto me void, but it shall accomplish that which I please, and it shall prosper in the thing, whereto I sent it.**"

God wants you to live the life of abundance that He has provided for you through the Lord Jesus Christ but you must be willing to yield what you have to God so that he can multiply it. God wants us to be cheerful givers. He does not want us to grumble or complain about giving.

Seed planting and harvest is an unchangeable law of the kingdom of God that always works. Whenever you sow, you can expect to receive a harvest. That is if you are sowing into good ground. It is imperative that you understand the seasons of seedtime and harvest. A lot of Christians get discouraged when he or she sows a seed, and they don't get an immediate harvest. Sometimes your harvest may come quickly, but sometimes it may take a while. But rest assured that it will come in due season.

The bible makes several references of the comparison of sowing seeds spiritually to a farmer sowing seeds naturally. Jesus taught us about sowing and reaping in Mark 4: 26-32

"So is the kingdom of God, as if a man should cast seed into the ground. And should sleep, and rise night and day, and the seed should spring and grow up, he knoweth not how. For the earth bringeth forth fruit of herself: first the blade, then the ear, after that the full corn in the ear."

Just as a farmer can expect results from the seeds he has planted, we can expect a harvest from the seeds, we have planted. But we must adhere to the process.

When it comes to natural things, seasons are important, so it is with spiritual things. There is a process that you must adhere to it you expect results. The first thing that you must do is:

Prepare the soil-Just as a farmer must get the soil ready before he can plant his seeds, we must get the soil of our heart ready before we can plant seeds. I write scriptures down on index cards so that I can meditate on them throughout the day and night.

Plant the seed-Once you have prepared the soil of your heart by meditating on the word of God, you should plant your seed. You plant your seed through praying the prayer of faith. You make your request known unto God and believe that you will receive what you have asked for. The next step is to take action by planting the material representation of that seed in the form of a gift. One of the things that I do is to bless my seed.

Water the seed-Continuous water the seed by reading the word of God and confessing the word of God.

Keep the weeds out-You keep the weeds out by holding on to your confession before the Lord.

Don't rob God. Give Him the first fruit of your increase. Proverbs 3:9-10 says "Honor the Lord with thy substance, and with thy first fruits of all thine increase. So shall thy barns be filled with plenty, and thy presses shall burst out with new wine"

Discussion Questions

1. Discuss the blessings that God promises to give to you if you fully obey his commands and give your tithes.

_____

_____

_____

_____

_____

_____

_____

_____

_____

_____

_____

_____

_____

_____

_____

_____

_____

_____

_____

_____

_____

_____

_____

_____

_____

_____

_____

_____

_____

_____

_____

_____

_____

2. Discuss the reasons that you should tithe.

_____

_____

_____

_____

_____

_____

_____

_____

_____

_____

_____

_____

_____

_____

_____

_____

_____

_____

_____

_____

_____

_____

_____

_____

_____

_____

_____

_____

_____

_____

3. Discuss how giving your tithe demonstrates your love for God.

_____

_____

_____

_____

_____

_____

_____

_____

_____

_____

_____

_____

_____

_____

_____

_____

_____

_____

_____

_____

_____

_____

_____

_____

_____

_____

_____

_____

_____

_____

_____

_____

_____

_____

_____

Fast to Last

Chapter 14

And when he had fasted forty days and forty nights,
he was afterward an hungred Matthew 4:2

Fasting is one of the most spiritual disciplines in the Christian life. In most cases, a spiritual fast involves abstaining from food while focusing on prayer. Fasting serves as an opportunity to deny your flesh so that the Spirit of God can take control and move in your life. It can serve as a tool to defeat Satan, our enemy. The last thing that Satan wants you to do is to fast because he knows that fasting tears down his strongholds and leads us to victory.

As a new believer, you might be asking the question in your mind, "why should I fast? What are the benefits of fasting? I am sure that you will have your own personal reason for fasting, but I can tell you that for whatever that you chose to fast, there will be great benefits. Some of the benefits of fasting are:

- Fasting helps build Godly character.
- Fasting teaches us to be more sensitive to the voice of God.
- Fasting helps you deny your flesh and places it under the submission of the Spirit of God.
- Fasting helps you to break free from any type of bondage that you are under.

There are a number of reasons why people fast. The reasons can range from fasting to get closer to God, for spiritual renewal, healing, guidance in making a decision, resolution to a problem or grace to handle a difficult situation. It could be a number of reasons why a person might fast. The bible gives us several examples of people who fasted for various reasons. Here are a few examples:

- David fasted when he was mourning the loss of his child. "2 Samuel chapter 12: 1-23
- Moses fasted for 40 days when he went up to the mountain to receive the commandments of God written on stone tablets. (Deuteronomy 9:9-18)
- Ezra fasted while mourning over sin.—Ezra 10:6-17
- Esther fasted for the safety of the Jews.—Esther 4:15-17
- Darius fasted for the safety of Daniel.—Daniel 6:18-23
- Daniel fasted for an answer to prayer.—Daniel 10:1-3
- Jesus fasted before temptation by Satan.—Matthew 4:1-2
- Paul fasted after his conversion.—Acts 9:1-9

For whatever reason that you decide to fast, you want to make sure that your time with the Lord is meaningful. The preparations that you make before you fast will determine how successful you will be. There are some steps or guidelines that you need to consider following in order to make your fast a rewarding experience. The first issue that you need to address is **setting your objective**: In other words you need to decide **why are you fasting**? Are you fasting because you have an issue that you need clarity on? Are fasting for an answer to prayer, perhaps healing in your body? Are you fasting because you want to draw closer to God? Are you fasting for the salvation of a loved one?

Secondly, you need to **determine the type of fast you will go on and how long you will fast**. There are many types of fasts:

1. Absolute Fast-This is a fast where you eliminate all food and water. This is the most severe fast, used mostly for the most serious cases.
2. Normal Fast-During this fast you will eliminate all solid foods and drink only liquids or selected meals.
3. Partial Fast-In this fast, you eliminate certain liquids or certain solids, but not all solids and liquids.

4. John Wesley Fast-This fast consists of eating only whole grain bread and water for ten days in preparation for a Christian service.
5. Rotation Fast-This fast allows you to eat only one of the six food groups each day for six days for medical purposes.
6. Supernatural Fast-This is a fast of no water or food for forty days. I would not recommend that you do this fast unless God has specifically instructed you to do so.

The next step is decide is how long will you fast? Decide if you will fast for one meal, one day, a week or several weeks. (I would recommend that as a beginner, you start off slow).

During the times that you are fasting from food, a good question to address is to what physical or social activities will you restrict yourself from? During the times that I fast, I often will not use social media such as Facebook, Twitter etc. I do that because sometimes Facebook can pose as a distraction to me. I want to make certain that I keep my mind free to focus on what God is saying to me. I can't do that if I am engaged in things that will distract me.

Another important step that you need to address is deciding what scriptures you will read. The reason that I am fasting determines the scriptures that I focus on during my fast. If I am fasting because I need healing in my body, then I find scriptures about healing in the Bible and I meditate on those scriptures. I highly recommend that you do the same.

Preparing your body physically is the next step. This is a very important step. Physical preparation makes the drastic change in your eating routine a little easier so that you can turn your full attention to the Lord in prayer. Some key things that you should do to make certain that your body is physically prepared is to:

- Consult your physician first, especially if you take prescription medication or have a chronic aliment.
- Do not rush into your fast.
- Prepare your body. Eat smaller meals before starting a fast. Avoid high-fat and sugary foods.
- Eat raw fruit and vegetables for two days before starting a fast.

Just as you must prepare yourself physically you must also prepare yourself spiritually. Your heart and mind must be spiritually prepared if you are going to be successful on your fast. If you have any unconfessed sins in your heart, you need to repent of them before you begin your fast. Unconfessed sins will hinder your prayer and the results of your fast. To being preparation, you should:

- Ask God to help you make a comprehensive list of your sins both those you are aware of and those you are not aware of.
- Confess every sin that the Holy Spirit calls to your remembrance and accept God's forgiveness (1 John 1:9).
- Seek forgiveness from all whom you have offended, and forgive all who have hurt you (Mark 11:25; Luke 11:4; 17:3, 4).
- Ask God to fill you with His Holy Spirit according to His command in Ephesians 5:18.
- Surrender your life fully to Jesus Christ as your Lord and Master; refuse to obey your worldly nature (Romans 12:1,2).
- Meditate on the attributes of God, His love, sovereignty, power, wisdom, faithfulness, grace, compassion, and others (Psalm 48:9,10; 103:1-8, 11-13).
- Begin your time of fasting and prayer with an expectant heart (Hebrews 11:6).

Do not underestimate spiritual opposition. Satan sometimes intensifies the natural battle between body and spirit (Galatians 5:16, 17).

Now that you have completed the necessary preparations by deciding the type and duration of your fast, and you have prepared yourself physically and spiritually, you are now ready to begin your fast. During your fast time, you should remain committed to praying and seeking God through reading His word. It is easy to let your mind wander and start to think about other things especially during your prayer time, but you must use discipline and keep your mind on God. Eliminate any and all things that will pose as a distraction to you. If something that is causing you not to be able to keep your flesh under subjection, then you need to refrain from doing it. It may mean that you need to get away from everyone while you are fasting. If that is the case for you, then if at all possible you do that. I encourage you to do whatever it takes for you to be successful.

Below are some practical points that you need to bear in mind:

- Medication should be withdrawn only with your physician's supervision.
- Limit your activity. Exercise only moderately.
- Rest as much as possible.
- Expect some physical discomforts such as hunger pains, dizziness, headache as a result of withdrawal from caffeine and sugar.
- The first two or three days are usually the hardest, but hold steady it gets easier as time passes by.
- When your designated time for fasting is completed, use wisdom as you begin to eat again. How you break your fast is extremely important for both your physical and spiritual wellbeing. Don't gorge yourself with all the food you missed while you were fasting. You should being gradually.

What to Expect After Your Fast

At the end of your fast, you should be in expectation of seeing results. Your faith and confidence in the Lord should be strengthened. You should feel mentally, spiritually and physically refreshed.

It is important to realize that a single fast is not a one time around spiritual cure all. You will need to continue to fast on a regular basis.

It is my prayer that you will be successful during your fast, but if you are not please don't be discouraged and by all means don't give up on the idea of fasting. Take the time to revisit the situation, circumstances or events that might have caused your failure. For example if you were tempted by the foods advertisements on television, then perhaps you should eliminate watching television during the time that you are fasting.

Angela Camon

Discussion Questions

1. What some of the benefits of fasting?

2. Give Biblical examples of people who fasted.

_____

_____

_____

_____

_____

_____

_____

_____

_____

_____

_____

_____

_____

_____

_____

_____

_____

_____

_____

_____

_____

_____

_____

_____

_____

_____

_____

_____

_____

_____

_____

_____

3. Discuss the various types of fasts.

4. How should you prepare physically and spiritually before you begin a fast?

_____

_____

_____

_____

_____

_____

_____

_____

_____

_____

_____

_____

_____

_____

_____

_____

_____

_____

_____

_____

_____

_____

_____

_____

_____

_____

_____

_____

_____

_____

_____

_____

Let Your Light Shine
Chapter 15

Let your light so shine before men, that they may see your good works, and glorify your Father which is in heaven. Matthew 5:16

As a new believer, it is so important to let your light shine. In so many cases, the only bible that some people will ever read is the life that you live. People may never pick up the bible and read it, but they will make judgments and decisions about their lives based on how you live your life. That is why we need to make sure our lives are worth reading about. By the grace of God, we must reflect the Word and truth of God in the way we live our lives and conduct our affairs. People are always watching us to see if we are living a life that exemplifies a true child of God. Your attitude and Christian example must attract people to your lifestyle. They must see by your example that you are committed to the Lord. If you are filled with the Holy Spirit, then the fruit of the Spirit will be visible in your life.

I have encountered people who have given me a litany of excuses as to why they don't attend church, but one that I often hear the most is "nobody in the church is right". Of course that is an unfair statement to make because there are some true Christians who are living a holy and acceptable life unto God. However, there is some validity to what has been said, there are some people who live a hypocritical life. They say one thing and do another. Many people call themselves Christians, but they are not living the life of a Christian. They claim to know Jesus and confess that they have submitted a surrendered life to him, but yet they follow the pattern of the world. That is one example of being a hypocrite.

We must practice what we preach. As Christians we cannot have the "do as I say, not as I do mentality, but we must be committed to living a Godly life every day. The testimony of your life must be consistent with your words. The Word of God says "Whosoever obeys the commandments and teach others to do the same will be great in the kingdom of heaven (Matthew 5:19). We first must obey before we can teach others. One of the worst things that we can do is to preach what we don't practice. If we live our lives contrary to our testimony, we can't be effective witnesses.

In Matthew 5th chapter Jesus refers to as believers as the salt of the earth. We have been called to make a difference in the world and leave a lasting impact in the lives of people around us. Our spiritual influence should bring a different flavor to a situation and relationships and to the world as a whole. The power of our influence will be determined by the character of our lives.

The Bible gives a description of what our character should be like. Our Christian duty is similar to the functions and purposes that salt has.

1. **We know that salt is used as a preservative.** It is used to preserve foods. As children of God we are to preserve our communities to keep society from going into corruption. We see a lot of things going on in our communities, and we must stand up and teach the Word of God.

2. **Salt seasons or adds flavor**. You know how some foods are bland. They need a little salt to bring out the flavor of the food. It wakes those taste buds up. So it is with us, we should bring out the best and add zest and flavor to life.

3. **Salt is used to heal wounds**-There are many people who are hurting. They have emotional wounds, physical wounds, mental and spiritual wounds. They are waiting for someone to give them an encouraging word to heal their broken heart.

4. **Salt is vital to life**-Salt regulates the water in our cells, it aids in muscle contraction, nerve impulses and heartbeats. Without vital salt, we would die. We as Christians are vital to the world. We are life line to somebody getting saved or guiding someone as they walk into their destiny.

5. **Salt make things pure**-Let's take a look at 2Kings 2:20-22. "And he said, Bring me a new cruse, and put salt therein. And

they brought *it* to him. And he went forth unto the spring of the waters, and cast the salt in there, and said, Thus saith the LORD, I have healed these waters; there shall not be from thence any more death or barren *land*. So the waters were healed unto this day, according to the saying of Elisha which he spake. This scripture talks about Elisha healing Jericho waters. The men of the city had told Elisha the city is pleasant but the water is bad. Elisha said "bring me a new cruse and put salt in it. Elisha went to the spring and put salt in it. The Lord healed the water. We have to pour what is inside of us to make the world pure. See we have the Holy Ghost living on the inside of us. We have to be pure. Have a pure mind. Philippians 4:8 says "Finally, brethren, whatsoever things are true, whatsoever things are honest, whatsoever things are just, whatsoever things are pure, whatsoever things are lovely, whatsoever things are of good report; if there be any virtue, and if there be any praise, think on these things".

Think on these things so you will keep a pure mind. That why you have to careful what you watch on television. Be careful what you log into on the internet. See you can't allow anything to sever your connection to Jesus.

6. **Salt is like peroxide**. It is an antiseptic. It kills germs. We act the same way. When we see a messy situation or when we see a person living in sin, we are to help them clean their lives up. Clean those cuts and bruises that we sometimes get in life.

7. **Salt melts and softens**. I am quite sure those in who live in areas where it snows during the winter time, appreciates the benefit that salt gives in melting the ice away. Salt also softens hard water.

That is the way it should be with our speech. Proverbs 15:1 says "A soft answer turneth away wrath, but grievous words stir up anger. Colossians 4:6 "Let your speech be always with grace, seasoned with the salt, that ye may know how ye ought to answer every man".

Our words should be tender and soft. We should use words that bring healing. The phrase seasoned with salt means seasoned with grace and wisdom. We should be careful of the words that come out of our mouth.

If we live Godly lives others will want to follow us simply because they want what we have. I can remember a friend telling me about a lady on her job who was so mean to her. Every day she did all she could to try to make my friend upset. The more she tried to make her upset, the more my friend prayed for the lady. My friend continued to display her Christian disposition. This went on for a period of time, but eventually, the lady came to my friend and told her why she gave her a hard time. She said "every time you come to work you always have a smile on your face. I don't understand how you could come to work so happy every day, while everyone else is so miserable with all the problems on the job. The lady confessed that she wanted my friend to be miserable, so she purposely treated her bad in any way that she could. The lady told my friend "it didn't matter how bad I treated you though you always treated me nice". She said "I don't understand how you could do that, but I want to understand. That day my friend led that woman to Christ. Not only did she lead that lady to Christ, but she led so many others just by letting her light shine. Think for a moment: what if my friend had decided not to let her light shine? What if she had retaliated against the lady on her job? That situation would have had a different outcome.

Not only is living an exemplary life before others important, but sharing your testimony is also beneficial in helping draw others to Christ. Your testimony is evidence of what God has done in your life. It is a look back at where you have come from and where you are now. It is a story of how your life was before you accepted Christ. Every Christian has a testimony and every testimony is significant. Your testimony may consist of being delivered from a life of drug/alcohol addiction, prostitution, gambling addiction, while another Christian may have grown up in a Christian home and never experienced that type of lifestyle. The fact of the matter is we were all sinners separated from God and our on way to hell. It is because of God's grace that we even have a testimony to share.

Your testimony has power. Revelation 12:11 says, "And they overcame by the blood of the Lamb and the word of their testimony, and they loved not their lives unto the death".

Sharing your testimony is a key element in winning souls for Christ. By sharing, many people who are facing situations that seem hopeless will discover that there is hope through Jesus Christ. Somebody needs to hear your testimony so that they will be inspired to seek God for themselves. Then they can experience the peace and satisfaction that comes along with having a relationship with Jesus. The more you share and talk about how God has intervened in your life, the more people will began to realize that God is real, miracles do happen and prayer works. Not only will sharing your testimony offer encouragement to the sinner, it will give an opportunity to reflect on what God has done in your life. Sharing with unbelievers is what we as believers have been called to do. God has given us the privilege of being His ambassadors so we should consider it an honor to share our testimony.

Some people are ashamed to tell the things that God has delivered them from. I have a friend of mine who readily admits that she does not feel comfortable sharing her testimony because she is embarrassed about some of the things that she had done in the past. She felt like she was being a hypocrite by telling others about sinning against God, when she in fact had sinned against Him for so many years. She didn't think it was her place to tell others about their sins. I explained to my friend that she was falling right into the enemy's trap. My friend has such an awesome testimony and Satan knows that if she shares her story, that others will be delivered and set free. So he deceived her into thinking that she was being hypocritical in sharing about her life. My friend, don't allow Satan to trick you into the carry a load of guilt and shame about your past. Your past is just that . . . . the past. Instead of focusing on what you used to do, focus on what you can do for Christ with your life now and that includes letting your light shine and sharing your testimony.

Discussion Questions

1. As a new born again believer, why is it important to let your light shine?

_____

_____

_____

_____

_____

_____

_____

_____

_____

_____

_____

_____

_____

_____

_____

_____

_____

_____

_____

_____

_____

_____

_____

_____

_____

_____

_____

_____

_____

_____

2. Discuss what Jesus means when he refers to believers as the salt of the earth.

_____

_____

_____

_____

_____

_____

_____

_____

_____

_____

_____

_____

_____

_____

_____

_____

_____

_____

_____

_____

_____

_____

_____

_____

_____

_____

_____

_____

_____

_____

_____

_____

_____

3. Discuss some ways of letting your light shine.

My Final Thoughts

My friend, if you have been searching and seeking trying to satisfy your sense of fulfillment with the things of the world, let me encourage you to stop trying it because it won't work. You can't fill your life with things such as material possessions with the expectation that those things will do only what a relationship with God will do. The only way to fill that empty and lonely void in your life is through a relationship with Jesus.

If you have not accepted Jesus as your Lord and Savior or ever had the pleasure of being in a relationship with him and experiencing true fellowship with him, I pray that after reading this book, you will now see the benefit of having Him as Savior and will accept His offer of salvation. This will be by far the greatest decision that you will ever have to make in your life. It is also the most important because it is the only decision that determines your destiny of heaven or hell.

As you continue on your Christian journey, it is my prayer that you will be inspired to use the tools and strategies mentioned throughout this book so that you can continue to grow and enjoy the benefits that this new life in Christ has to offer. You are a new creation. *Therefore if any man be in Christ, he is a new creature: old things are passed away; behold, all things are become new (2 Corinthians 5:17).* You are no longer defined by the old things that have passed away but rather by the new things that come from God.